Painting Churches

by Tina Howe

SAMUEL FRENCH, INC.

45 WEST 25TH STREET   NEW YORK 10010
7623 SUNSET BOULEVARD   HOLLYWOOD 90046
LONDON   *TORONTO*

THE SECOND STAGE

A Non-Profit Theatre Organization

Robyn Goodman and Carole Rothman
Artistic Directors

Presents

PAINTING CHURCHES

by
TINA HOWE

Directed by
CAROLE ROTHMAN

Starring

FRANCES CONROY   **DONALD MOFFAT**   **MARIAN SELDES**

Set Design
HEIDI LANDESMAN

Lighting Design
FRANCES ARONSON

Costume Design
NAN CIBULA

Sound Design
GARY HARRIS

Hair Design
ANTONIO SODDU

Production Stage Manager
LORETTA ROBERTSON

Stage Manager
NANCY KOHLBECK

Production Supervisor for The Second Stage: KIM NOVICK

CASTING BY SIMON AND KUMIN
MEG SIMON AND FRAN KUMIN

This production is made possible in part with public funds from the New York State Council on the Arts and the National Endowment for the Arts.

4

Fanny Church . . . . MARIAN SELDES

Gardner Church . . . . DONALD MOFFAT

Margaret Church . . . . FRANCES CONROY

PLACE: Beacon Hill—Boston, Mass.

TIME: A few years ago.

ACT I	Scene 1:	A bright spring morning
	Scene 2:	2 days later
	Scene 3:	24 hours later
ACT II	Scene 1:	3 days later
	Scene 2:	The last day

There will be one intermission

The Second Stage is a member of the Alliance of Resident Theatres—NY

5

LAMB'S THEATRE

ELIZABETH I. McCANN   NELLE NUGENT   RAY LARSEN
LEE GUBER   SHELLY GROSS

present

THE SECOND STAGE PRODUCTION

of

PAINTING CHURCHES

by

TINA HOWE

starring

GEORGE N. ELIZABETH MARIAN
MARTIN McGOVERN SELDES

Setting by   Costumes by   Lighting by
HEIDI LANDESMAN   LINDA FISHER   FRANCES ARONSON

Directed by

CAROLE ROTHMAN

PAINTING CHURCHES opened at the Lamb's
Theatre on November 22, 1983.

CAST

(in order of appearance)

Fanny Church .... MARIAN SELDES

Gardner Church .... GEORGE N. MARTIN

Margaret Church .... ELIZABETH McGOVERN

PLACE: Beacon Hill — Boston, Mass.

ACT I

Scene 1: A bright spring morning

Scene 2: 2 days later

Scene 3: 24 hours later

ACT II

Scene 1: 3 days later

Scene 2: The last day

THERE WILL BE ONE INTERMISSION.

STANDBYS

Standbys never substitute for listed players unless a specific announcement
for the appearance is made at the time of the performance.

Standbys for Fanny Church—Lily Lodge; Standby for Gardner Church—Wyman Pendleton;
Standby for Margaret Church—Frances McDormand.

7

CHARACTERS

FANNY SEDGWICK CHURCH — A Bostonian from a fine old family, in her 60's.

GARDNER CHURCH — Her husband, an eminent New England poet from a finer family, in his 70's.

MARGARET CHURCH (MAGS) — Their daughter, a painter, in her early 30's.

Painting Churches

ACT ONE

Scene 1

*The living room of the Church's townhouse on Beacon
Hill one week before everything will be moved to
Cape Cod. Empty packing cartons line the room
and all the furniture has been tagged with brightly
colored markers. At first glance it looks like any
discreet Boston interior, but on closer scrutiny one
notices a certain flamboyance. Oddities from second hand stores are mixed in with the fine old furniture and exotic hand made curios vie with tasteful
family objets d'art. What makes the room remarkable though, is the play of light that pours through
three soaring arched windows. At one hour it's
hard-edged and brilliant, the next, it's dappled and
yielding. It transforms whatever it touches giving
the room a distinct feeling of unreality. It's several
years ago, a bright spring morning.*

*FANNY is sitting on the sofa wrapping a valuable old
silver coffee service. She's wearing a worn bathrobe
and fashionable hat. As she works, she makes a list
of everything on a yellow legal pad. GARDNER
can be heard typing in his study down the hall.*

FANNY. (*She picks up a coffee pot.*) God, this is good
looking! I'd forgotten how handsome Mama's old silver
was! It's probably worth a fortune. It certainly weighs
enough! (*calling out*) GARRRRRRRRRRRRRRRRRRRD-
NERRRRRRRRRRRR . . . ? Well, it should bring us a

9

pretty penny, that's for sure. (*Wraps it, places it in a carton and then picks up the tray that goes with it. She holds it up like a mirror and adjusts her hat; louder in another register.*) OH GARRRRRRRRRRRRRRRRD-NERRRRR . . . ? (*He continues typing. She then reaches for a small box and opens it with reverence.*) Grandma's Paul Revere tea spoons . . . ! (*She takes several out and fondles them.*) I don't care how desperate things get, these will never go! One has to maintain some standards! (*She writes on her list.*) "Grandma's Paul Revere tea spoons, Cotuit!" . . . WASN'T IT THE AMERICAN WING OF THE METROPOLITAN MUSEUM OF ART THAT WANTED GRANDMA'S PAUL REVERE TEA SPOONS SO BADLY . . . ? (*She looks at her reflection in the tray again.*) This is a very good looking hat, if I do say so. I was awfully smart to grab it up. (*silence*) DON'T YOU REMEM-BER A DISTINGUISHED LOOKING MAN COM-ING TO THE HOUSE AND OFFERING US $50,000 FOR GRANDMA'S PAUL REVERE TEA SPOONS . . . ? HE HAD ON THESE MARVELOUS SHOES! THEY WERE SO POINTED AT THE ENDS WE COULDN'T IMAGINE HOW HE EVER GOT THEM ON AND THEY WERE SHINED TO WITHIN AN INCH OF THEIR LIVES AND I REMEMBER HIM SAYING HE CAME FROM THE . . . AMERI-CAN WING OF THE METROPOLITAN MUSEUM OF ART! . . . HELLO? . . . GARDNER . . . ? ARE YOU THERE! (*The typing stops.*) YOO HOOOO-OOO . . . (*like a fog horn*) GARRRRRRRRRRRD-NERRRRRRR . . . ?

GARDNER. (*offstage; from his study*) YES DEAR . . . IS THAT YOU . . . ?

FANNY. OF COURSE IT'S ME! WHO ELSE COULD IT POSSIBLY BE . . . ? DARLING, PLEASE COME HERE FOR A MINUTE. (*The typing resumes.*) FOR GOD'S SAKE, WILL YOU STOP THAT DREADFUL TYPING BEFORE YOU SEND ME STRAIGHT TO THE NUT HOUSE . . . ? (*in a new register*) GARRR-RRRRRRRRRRDNERRRRRR . . . ? (*He stops.*)

GARDNER. (*offstage)* WHAT'S THAT? MAGS IS BACK FROM THE NUT HOUSE . . . ? (*brief silence*) I'LL BE WITH YOU IN A MOMENT, I DIDN'T HEAR HER RING. (*He starts singing the refrain of "Nothing Could be Finer."**)	FANNY. I SAID . . . Lord, I hate this yelling . . . PLEASE . . . COME . . . HERE! It's a wonder I'm not in a straight jacket already. Actually, it might be rather nice for a change . . . Peaceful. DARLING . . . I WANT TO SHOW YOU MY NEW HAT!

(*Silence, GARDNER enters, still singing. He's wearing mis-matched tweeds and is holding a stack of papers which keep drifting to the floor.*)

GARDNER. Oh, don't you look nice! Very attractive, very attractive!

FANNY. But I'm still in my bathrobe.

GARDNER. (*looking around the room, leaking more papers*) Well, where's Mags?

---

*Note: Permission to produce *Painting Churches* does not include permission to use this song, which ought to be procured from the copyright owner.

FANNY. Darling, you're dropping your papers all over the floor.

GARDNER. (*spies the silver tray*) I remember this! Aunt Alice gave it to us, didn't she? (*He picks it up.*) Good Lord, it's heavy. What's it made of? Lead?!

FANNY. No, Aunt Alice did *not* give it to us. It was Mama's.

GARDNER. Oh yes . . . (*He starts to exit with it.*)

FANNY. Could I have it back, please?

GARDNER. (*hands it to her, dropping more papers*) Oh, sure thing . . . Where's Mags? I thought you said she was here.

FANNY. I didn't say Mags was here, I asked *you* to come here.

GARDNER. (*papers spilling*) Damned papers keep falling . . .

FANNY. I wanted to show you my new hat. I bought it in honor of Mags' visit. Isn't it marvelous?

GARDNER. (*picking up the papers as more drop*) Yes, yes, very nice . . .

FANNY. Gardner, you're not even looking at it!

GARDNER. Very becoming . . .

FANNY. You don't think it's too bright, do you? I don't want to look like a traffic light. Guess how much it cost?

GARDNER. (*A whole sheaf of papers slides to the floor, he dives for them.*) OH SHIT!

FANNY. (*gets to them first*) It's alright, I've got them, I've got them. (*She hands them to him.*)

GARDNER. You'd think they had wings on them . . .

FANNY. Here you   GARDNER. . . . damned
go . . .   things won't hold still!

FANNY. Gar . . . ?

GARDNER. (*has become engrossed in one of the pages and is lost reading it*) Mmmmm?

FANNY. HELLO?

GARDNER. (*startled*) What's that?

FANNY. (*in a whisper*) My hat. Guess how much it cost.

GARDNER. Oh yes. Let's see . . . $10?

FANNY. $10? . . . IS THAT ALL . . . ?

GARDNER. 20?

FANNY. GARDNER, THIS HAPPENS TO BE A DESIGNER HAT! DESIGNER HATS START AT $50 . . . 75!

GARDNER. (*jumps*) Was that the door bell?

FANNY. No, it wasn't the door bell. Though it's high time Mags were here. She was probably in a train wreck!

GARDNER. (*looking through his papers*) I'm beginning to get fond of Wallace Stevens again.

FANNY. This damned move is going to kill me! Send me straight to my grave!

GARDNER. (*reading from a page*)
"The mules that angels ride come slowly down
The blazing passes, from beyond the sun.
Descensions of their tinkling bells arrive.
These muleteers are dainty of their way . . ."
(*pause*) Don't you love that! "These muleteers are *dainty* of their way . . . !?"

FANNY. Gar, the hat. How much? (*GARDNER sighs.*)

FANNY. Darling . . . ?

GARDNER. Oh yes. Let's see . . . $50? 75?

FANNY. It's French.

GARDNER. 300!

FANNY. (*triumphant*) No, 85¢

GARDNER. 85¢! . . . I thought you said . . .

FANNY. That's right . . . eighty . . . five . . . *cents!*

GARDNER. Well, you sure had me fooled!

FANNY. I found it at the Thrift Shop.

GARDNER. I thought it cost at least $50 or 75. You know, designer hats are very expensive!

FANNY. It was on the mark-down table. (*She takes it off and shows him the label.*) See that? Lily Daché! When I saw that label, I nearly keeled over right into the fur coats!

GARDNER. (*handling it*) Well, what do you know, that's the same label that's in my bathrobe.

FANNY. Darling, Lily Daché designed hats, not men's bathrobes!

GARDNER. Yup . . . "Lily Daché" . . . same name . . .

FANNY. If you look again, I'm sure you'll see . . .

GARDNER. . . . same script, same color, same size. I'll show you. (*He exits.*)

FANNY. Poor lamb can't keep anything straight anymore. (*looks at herself in the tray again*) God, this is a good looking hat!

GARDNER. (*returns with a nondescript plaid bathrobe; he points to the label.*) See that . . . ? What does it say?

FANNY. (*refusing to look at it*) Lily Daché was a *hat* designer! She designed ladies' *hats!*

GARDNER. What . . . does . . . it . . . say?

FANNY. Gardner, you're being ridiculous.

GARDNER. (*forcing it on her*) Read . . . the label!

FANNY. Lily Daché did *not* design this bathrobe, I don't care what the label says!

GARDNER. READ! (*FANNY reads it.*) ALL RIGHT, NOW WHAT DOES IT SAY . . . ?

FANNY. (*chagrined*) Lily Daché.

GARDNER. I told you!

FANNY. Wait a minute, let me look at that again. (*She does, then throws the robe at him in disgust.*) Gar, Lily Daché never designed a bathrobe in her life! Someone obviously ripped the label off one of her hats and then sewed it into the robe.

GARDNER. (*puts it on over his jacket*) It's damned good looking. I've always loved this robe. I think you gave it to me . . . Well, I've got to get back to work. (*He abruptly exits.*)

FANNY. Where did you get that robe anyway? . . . I didn't give it to you, did I . . . ? (*Silence; he resumes typing. Holding the tray up again and admiring herself.*) You know, I think I *did* give it to him. I remember how excited I was when I found it at the Thrift Shop . . . 50¢ and never worn! *I* couldn't have sewn that label in to impress him, could I? . . . I can't be that far gone! . . . The poor lamb wouldn't even notice it, let alone understand its cachet . . . Uuuuuh, this damned tray is even heavier than the coffee pot. They must have been amazons in the old days! (*writes on her pad*) "Empire tray, Parke Bernet Galleries," and good riddance! (*She wraps it and drops it into the carton with the coffee pot.*) Where *is* that wretched Mags? It would be just like her to get into a train wreck! She was supposed to be here hours ago. Well, if she doesn't show up soon, I'm going to drop dead of exhaustion. God, wouldn't that be wonderful? . . . Then they could just cart me off into storage with all the old chandeliers and china . . . (*The door bell rings.*)

FANNY. IT'S MAGS, IT'S MAGS!	GARDNER. (*offstage*) COMING, COMING

(*a pause; dashing* . . . I'VE GOT IT . . .
out of the room, . . . COMING! (*dash-*
colliding into GARD- *into the room, colliding*
NER) GOOD GOD, *into FANNY*) I'VE GOT
LOOK AT ME! I'M IT . . . HOLD ON . . .
STILL IN MY BATH- COMING . . .
ROBE! COMING . . .

FANNY. (*offstage*) MAGS IS HERE! IT'S
MAGS . . . SHE'S FINALLY HERE!

(*GARDNER exits to open the front door. MAGS comes*
staggering in carrying a suitcase and enormous duf-
fle bag. She wears wonderfully distinctive clothes
and has very much her own look. She's extremely
out of breath and too wrought up to drop her heavy
bags.)

MAGS. I'm sorry . . . I'm sorry I'm so late . . . Everything went wrong! A passenger had a heart attack outside of New London and we had to stop . . . It was ter-
rifying! All these medics and policemen came swarming
onto the train and the conductor kept running up and
down the aisles telling everyone not to leave their seats
under any circumstances . . . Then the New London
fire department came screeching down to the tracks,
sirens blaring, lights whirling, and all these men in black
rubber suits started pouring through the doors . . . *That*
took two hours . . .

FANNY. (*offstage*) DARLING . . . DARLING . . .
WHERE ARE YOU . . . ?

MAGS. *Then,* I couldn't get a cab at the station. There
just weren't any! I must have circled the block 15 times.
Finally I just stepped out into the traffic with my thumb

out, but no one would pick me up . . . so I walked . . .

FANNY. (*offstage*) Damned zipper's stuck . . .

GARDNER. You walked all the way from the South Station?

MAGS. Well actually, I ran . . .

GARDNER. You had poor Mum scared to death.

MAGS. (*finally puts the bags down with a deep sigh*) I'm sorry . . . I'm really sorry. It was a nightmare.

FANNY. (*Re-enters the room, her dress over her head. The zipper's stuck, she staggers around blindly.*) Damned zipper! Gar, will you please help me with this?

MAGS. (*squeezing him tight*) Oh Daddy . . . Daddy!

GARDNER. My Mags!

MAGS. I never thought I'd get here! . . . Oh, you look wonderful!

GARDNER. Well, you don't look so bad yourself!

MAGS. I love your hair. It's gotten so . . . white!

FANNY. (*still lost in her dress, struggling with the zipper*) This is *so* typical . . . just as Mags arrives, my zipper has to break! (*FANNY grunts and struggles.*)

MAGS. (*waves at her*) Hi, Mum . . .

FANNY. Just a minute, dear, my zipper's . . .

GARDNER. (*picks up MAGS' bags*) Well, sit down and take a load off your feet . . .

MAGS. I was so afraid I'd never make it . . .

GARDNER. (*staggering under the weight of her bags*) What have you got in here? Lead weights?

MAGS. I can't believe you're finally letting me do you.

FANNY. (*flings her arms around MAGS, practically knocking her over*) OH, DARLING . . . MY PRECIOUS MAGS, YOU'RE HERE

GARDNER. (*lurching around in circles*) Now let's see . . . where should I put these. . . ?

AT LAST

FANNY. I was sure your train had derailed and you were lying dead in some ditch!

MAGS. (*pulls away from FANNY to come to GARDNER's rescue*) Daddy, please, let me . . . these are much too heavy.

FANNY. (*finally noticing MAGS*) GOOD LORD, WHAT HAVE YOU DONE TO YOUR HAIR?!

MAGS. (*struggling to take the bags from GARDNER*) Come on, give them to me . . . please? (*She sets them down by the sofa.*)

FANNY. (*as her dress starts to slide off one shoulder*) Oh, not again! . . . Gar, would you give me a hand and see what's wrong with this zipper. One minute it's stuck, the next it's falling to pieces. (*GARDNER goes to her and starts fussing with it.*)

MAGS. (*pacing*) I don't know, it's been crazy all week. Monday, I forgot to keep an appointment I'd made with a new model . . . Tuesday, I overslept and stood up my advanced painting students . . . Wednesday, the day of my meeting with Max Zoll, I forgot to put on my underpants . . .

FANNY. GODDAMNIT, GAR, CAN'T YOU DO ANYTHING ABOUT THIS ZIPPER?!

MAGS. I mean, there I was, racing down Broome Street in this gauzy Tibetan skirt when I tripped and fell right at his feet . . . SPLATT! My skirt goes flying over my head and there I am . . . everything staring him in the face . . .

FANNY. COME ON, GAR, USE A LITTLE MUSCLE!

MAGS. (*laughing*) Oh well, all that matters is that I finally got here . . . I mean . . . there you are . . .

GARDNER. (*struggling with the zipper*) I can't see it, it's too small!

FANNY. (*whirls away from GARDNER, pulling her dress off altogether*) OH FORGET IT! JUST FORGET IT! . . . The trolly's probably missing half its teeth, just like someone else I know. (*to MAGS*) I grind my teeth in my sleep now, I've worn them all down to stubs. Look at that! (*She flings open her mouth and points.*) Nothing left but the gums!

GARDNER. I never hear you grind your teeth . . .

FANNY. That's because I'm snoring so loud. How could you hear anything through all that racket? It even wakes me up. It's no wonder poor Daddy has to sleep downstairs.

MAGS. (*looking around*) Jeez, look at the place! So, you're finally doing it . . . selling the house and moving to Cotuit year round. I don't believe it. I just don't believe it!

GARDNER. Well, how about a drink to celebrate Mags' arrival?

MAGS. You've been here so long. Why move now?

FANNY. Gardner, what are you wearing that bathrobe for . . . ?

MAGS. You can't move. I won't let you!

FANNY. (*softly to GARDNER*) Really darling, you ought to pay more attention to your appearance.

MAGS. You love this house. *I* love this house . . . This room . . . the light.

GARDNER. So, Mags, how about a little . . . (*He drinks from an imaginary glass.*) to wet your whistle?

FANNY. We can't start drinking now, it isn't even noon yet!

MAGS. I'm starving. I've got to get something to eat

before I collapse! (*She exits towards the kitchen.*)

FANNY. What *have* you done to your hair, dear? The color's so queer and all your nice curl is gone.

GARDNER. It looks to me as if she dyed it.

FANNY. Yes, that's it. You're absolutely right! It's a completely different color. She dyed it bright red! (*MAGS can be heard thumping and thudding through the ice box.*) NOW MAGS, I DON'T WANT YOU FILLING UP ON SNACKS . . . I'VE MADE A PERFECTLY BEAUTIFUL LEG OF LAMB FOR LUNCH! . . . HELLO? . . . DO YOU HEAR ME . . . ? (*to GARDNER*) No one in our family has *ever* had red hair, it's so common looking.

GARDNER. I like it. It brings out her eyes.

FANNY. WHY ON EARTH DID YOU DYE YOUR HAIR *RED,* OF ALL COLORS . . . ?!

MAGS. (*returns, eating saltines out of the box*) I didn't dye my hair, I just added some highlight.

FANNY. I suppose that's what your arty friends in New York do . . . dye their hair all the colors of the rainbow!

GARDNER. Well, it's damned attractive if you ask me . . . damned attractive! (*MAGS unzips her duffle bag and rummages around in it while eating the saltines.*)

FANNY. Darling, I told you not to bring a lot of stuff with you. We're trying to get rid of things.

MAGS. (*pulls out a folding easel and starts setting it up*) AAAAAHHHHHH, here it is. Isn't it a beauty? I bought it just for you!

FANNY. Please don't get crumbs all over the floor. Crystal was just here yesterday. It was her last time before we move.

MAGS. (*at her easel*) God, I can hardly wait! I can't believe you're finally letting me do you.

FANNY. "*Do*" us? . . . What *are* you talking about?

GARDNER. (*reaching for the saltines*) Hey, Mags, could I have a couple of those?

MAGS. (*tosses him the box*) Sure! (*to FANNY*) Your portrait.

GARDNER. Thanks. (*He starts munching on a handful.*)

FANNY. You're planning to paint our portrait now? While we're trying to move . . . ?

GARDNER. (*mouth full*) Mmmmm, I'd forgotten just how delicious saltines are!

MAGS. It's a perfect opportunity. There'll be no distractions, you'll be completely at my mercy. Also, you promised.

FANNY. I did?

MAGS. Yes, you did.

FANNY. Well, I must have been off my rocker.

MAGS. No, you said, "You can paint us, you can dip us in concrete, you can do anything you want with us, just so long as you help us get out of here!"

GARDNER. (*offering the box of saltines to FANNY*) You really ought to try some of these, Fan, they're absolutely delicious!

FANNY. (*taking a few*) Why, thank you.

MAGS. I figure we'll pack in the morning and you'll pose in the afternoons. It'll be a nice diversion.

FANNY. These *are* good!

GARDNER. Here, dig in . . . take some more.

MAGS. I have some wonderful news . . . amazing news! I wanted to wait til I got here to tell you. (*They eat their saltines, passing the box back and forth as*

MAGS speaks.) You'll die! Just fall over into the packing cartons and die! Are you ready . . . ? BRACE YOURSELVES . . . OK, HERE GOES . . . I'm being given a one woman show at one of the most important galleries in New York this fall. Me, Margaret Church, exhibited at Castelli's, 420 West Broadway . . . Can you believe it?! . . . MY PORTRAITS HANGING IN THE SAME ROOMS THAT HAVE SHOWN RAUSCHENBURG, JOHNS, WARHOL, KELLY, LICHTENSTEIN, STELLA, SERRA, ALL THE HEAVIES . . . It's incredible, beyond belief . . . I mean, at my age . . . Do you know how good you have to be to get in there? It's a miracle . . . an honest-to-God, star spangled miracle! (*pause*)

FANNY. (*mouth full*)	GARDNER. (*likewise*)
Oh, darling, that's wonderful. We're so happy for you!	No one deserves it more, no one deserves it more!

MAGS. Through some fluke, some of Castelli's people showed up at our last faculty show at Pratt and were knocked out . . .

FANNY. (*reaching for the box of saltines*) More, more . . .

MAGS. They said they hadn't seen anyone handle light like me since the French Impressionists. They said I was this weird blend of Pierre Bonnard, Mary Cassat and David Hockney . . .

GARDNER. (*swallowing his own mouthful*) I told you they were good.

MAGS. Also, no one's doing portraits these days. They're considered passé. I'm so out of it, I'm in.

GARDNER. Well, you're loaded with talent and always have been.

FANNY. She gets it all from Mama, you know. Her miniature of Henry James is still one of the main attractions at the Atheneum. Of course no woman of breeding could be a professional artist in her day. It simply wasn't done. But talk about talent . . . that woman had talent to burn!

MAGS. I want to do one of you for the show.

FANNY. Oh, do Daddy, he's the famous one.

MAGS. No, I want to do you both. I've always wanted to do you and now I've finally got a good excuse.

FANNY. It's high time somebody painted Daddy again! I'm sick to death of that dreadful portrait of him in the National Gallery they keep reproducing. He looks like an undertaker!

GARDNER. Well, I think you should just do Mum. She's never looked handsomer.

FANNY. Oh, come on, I'm a perfect fright and you know it.

MAGS. I want to do you both. Side by side. In this room. Something really classy. You look so great. Mum with her crazy hats and everything and you with that face. If I could just get you to hold still long enough and actually pose.

GARDNER. (*walking around, distracted*) Where are those papers I just had? God damnit, Fanny . . .

MAGS. I have the feeling it's either now or never.

GARDNER. I can't hold on to anything around here. (*He exits to his study.*)

MAGS. I've always wanted to do you. It would be such a challenge.

FANNY. (*pulling MAGS next to her onto the sofa*) I'm so glad you're finally here, Mags. I'm very worried about Daddy.

MAGS. Mummy, please. I just got here.

FANNY. He's getting quite gaga.

MAGS. Mummy . . . !

FANNY. You haven't seen him in almost a year. Two weeks ago he walked through the front door of the Codman's house, kissed Emily on the cheek and settled down in the maid's room, thinking he was home!

MAGS. Oh come on, you're exaggerating.

FANNY. He's as mad as a hatter and getting worse every day! It's this damned new book of his. He works on it around the clock. I've read some of it, and it doesn't make one word of sense, it's all at 6s and 7s . . .

GARDNER. (*poking his head back in the room, spies some of his papers on a table and grabs them*) Ahhh, here they are. (*and exits*)

FANNY. (*voice lowered*) Ever since this dry spell with his poetry, he's been frantic, absolutely . . . frantic!

MAGS. I hate it when you do this.

FANNY. I'm just trying to get you to face the facts around here.

MAGS. There's nothing wrong with him! He's just as sane as the next man. Even saner, if you ask me.

FANNY. You know what he's doing now? You couldn't guess in a million years! . . . He's writing criticism! Daddy! (*She laughs.*) Can you believe it? The man doesn't have one analytic bone in his body. His mind is a complete jumble and always has been! (*There's a loud crash from GARDNER's study.*)

GARDNER. (*offstage*) SHIT!

MAGS. He's abstracted . . . That's the way he is.

FANNY. He doesn't spend any time with me anymore. He just holes up in that filthy study with Toots. God, I hate that bird! Though actually they're quite cunning together. Daddy's teaching him Grey's Elegy. You ought to see them in there, Toots perched on top of Daddy's head, spouting out verse after verse . . . Daddy, tap tap tapping away on his typewriter. They're quite a pair.

GARDNER. (*pokes his head back in*) Have you seen that Stevens' poem I was reading before?

FANNY. (*long suffering*) NO, I HAVEN'T SEEN THAT STEVENS' POEM YOU WERE READING BEFORE . . . ! Things are getting very tight around here, in case you haven't noticed. Daddy's last Pulitzer didn't even cover our real estate tax, and now that he's too doddery to give readings anymore, that income is gone . . . (*suddenly handing MAGS the sugarbowl she'd been wrapping*) Mags, *do* take this sugarbowl. You can use it to serve tea to your students at that wretched art school of yours . . .

MAGS. It's called Pratt! The Pratt Institute.

FANNY. Pratt, Platt, whatever . . .

MAGS. And I don't serve tea to my students, I teach them how to paint.

FANNY. Well, I'm sure none of them has ever seen a sugarbowl as handsome as this before.

GARDNER. (*reappearing again*) You're sure you haven't seen it . . . ?

FANNY. (*loud and angry*) YES, I'M SURE I HAVEN'T SEEN IT! I JUST TOLD YOU I HAVEN'T SEEN IT!

GARDNER. (*retreating*) Right you are, right you are. (*He exits.*)

FANNY. God! (*silence*)

MAGS. What do you have to yell at him like that for?

FANNY. Because the poor thing's as deaf as an adder! (*MAGS sighs deeply; silence.*)

FANNY. (*suddenly exuberant, leads her over to a lamp*) Come, I want to show you something?

MAGS. (*looking at it*) What is it?

FANNY. Something I made. (*MAGS is about to turn it on.*) WAIT, DON'T TURN IT ON YET! It's got to be dark to get the full effect. (*She rushes to the windows and pulls down the shades.*)

MAGS. What *are* you doing . . . ?

FANNY. Hold your horses a minute. You'll see . . . (*as the room gets darker and darker*) Poor me, you wouldn't believe the lengths I go to to amuse myself these days . . .

MAGS. (*touching the lamp shade*) What is this? It looks like a scene of some sort.

FANNY. It's an invention I made . . . a kind of magic lantern.

MAGS. Gee . . . it's amazing . . .

FANNY. What I did was buy an old engraving of the Grand Canal . . .

MAGS. You *made* this?

FANNY. . . . and then color it in with crayons. Next, I got out my sewing scissors and cut out all the street lamps and windows . . . anything that light would shine through. Then I pasted it over a plain lampshade, put the shade on this old horror of a lamp, turned on the switch and . . . (*She turns it on.*) . . . VOILA . . . VENICE TWINKLING AT DUSK! It's quite effective, don't you think . . . ?

MAGS. (*walking around it*) Jeeez . . .

FANNY. And see, I poked out all the little lights on the gondolas with a straight pin.

MAGS. Where on earth did you get the idea?

FANNY. Well you know, idle minds . . . (*FANNY spins the shade, making the lights whirl.*)

MAGS. It's really amazing. I mean, you	GARDNER. (*enters*) HERE IT IS. IT WAS

you could sell this in a store!

RIGHT ON TOP OF MY DESK THE WHOLE TIME. (*He crashes into a table.*) OOOOOWWWWW!

FANNY. LOOK OUT, LOOK OUT!

MAGS. (*rushes over to him*) Oh, Daddy, are you all right!

FANNY. WATCH WHERE YOU'RE GOING, WATCH WHERE YOU'RE GOING!

GARDNER. (*hopping up and down on one leg*) GOD-DAMNIT! . . . I HIT MY SHIN!

FANNY. I was just showing Mags my lamp . . .

GARDNER. (*limping over to it*) Oh yes, isn't that something? Mum is awfully clever with that kind of thing . . . It was all her idea, the whole thing. Buying the engraving, coloring it in, cutting out all those little dots.

FANNY. Not "dots" . . . lights and windows, lights and windows!

GARDNER. Right, right . . . lights and windows.

FANNY. Well, we'd better get some light back in here before someone breaks their neck. (*She zaps the shades back up.*)

GARDNER. (*puts his arm around MAGS*) Gee, it's good to have you back.

MAGS. It's good to be back.

GARDNER. And I like that new red hair of yours. It's very becoming.

MAGS. But I told you, I hardly touched it . . .

GARDNER. Well, something's different. You've got a glow. So . . . how do you want us to pose for this grand portrait of yours . . . ? (*He poses self-consciously.*)

MAGS. Oh Daddy, setting up a portrait takes alot of time and thought. You've got to figure out the background, the lighting, what to wear, the sort of mood you want to . . .

FANNY. OOOOH, LET'S DRESS UP, LET'S DRESS UP! (*She grabs a packing blanket, drapes it around herself and links arms with GARDNER, striking an elegant pose.*) This *is* going to be fun. She was absolutely right! Come on, Gar, look distinguished!

MAGS. Mummy please, it's not a game!

FANNY. (*more and more excited*) You still have your tuxedo, don't you? And I'll wear my marvelous long black dress that makes me look like that fascinating woman in the Sargeant painting! (*She strikes the famous profile pose.*)

MAGS. MUMMY . . . ?!

FANNY. I'm sorry, we'll behave, just tell us what to do. (*They settle down next to each other.*)

GARDNER. That's right, you're the boss.

FANNY. Yes, you're the boss.

MAGS. But I'm not ready yet, I haven't set anything up.

FANNY. Relax, darling, we just want to get the hang of it . . .

(*They stare straight ahead, trying to look like suitable subjects, but they can't hold still. They keep making faces; lifting an eyebrow, wriggling a nose, twitching a lip, nothing grotesque, just flickering little changes; a half smile here, a self-important frown there. They steal glances at each other every so often.*)

GARDNER. How am I doing, Fan?

FANNY. Brilliantly, absolutely brilliantly!

MAGS. But you're making faces.

FANNY. *I'm* not making faces, (*turning to GARD-NER and making a face*) are *you* making faces, Gar?

GARDNER. (*instantly making one*) Certainly not! I'm the picture of restraint!

(*Without meaning to, they get sillier and sillier. They start giggling, then laughing.*)

MAGS. (*can't help but join in*) You two are impossible . . . completely impossible! I was crazy to think I could ever pull this off! (*laughing away*) Look at you . . . just . . . look at you!

BLACKOUT

SCENE 2

Two days later, around five in the afternoon. Half of the Church's household has been dragged into the living room for packing. Overflowing cartons are everywhere. They're filled with pots and pans, dishes and glasses, and the entire contents of two linen closets. MAGS has placed a stepladder under one of the windows. A pile of table cloths and curtains is flung beneath it. Two side chairs are in readiness for the eventual pose.

MAGS. (*Has just pulled a large crimson table cloth out of a carton. She unfurls it with one shimmering toss*) PERFECT . . . PERFECT . . . !

FANNY. (*seated on the sofa, clutches an old pair of galoshes to her chest*) Look at these old horrors, half the rubber is rotted away and the fasteners are falling to pieces . . . GARDNER . . . ? OH GARRRRRRRRRRD-NERRRRR . . . ?

MAGS. (*rippling out the table cloth with shorter snapping motions*) Have you ever seen such a color . . . ?

FANNY. I'VE FOUND YOUR OLD SLEDDING GALOSHES IN WITH THE POTS AND PANS. DO YOU STILL WANT THEM?

MAGS. It's like something out of a Rubens . . . ! (*She slings it over a chair and then sits on a foot stool to finish the Sara Lee banana cake she started. As she eats, she looks at the table cloth making happy grunting sounds.*)

FANNY. (*lovingly puts the galoshes on over her shoes and wiggles her feet*) God, these bring back memories! There were real snow storms in the old days. Not these pathetic little two inch droppings we have now. After a particularly heavy one, Daddy and I used to go sledding on the Common. This was way before you were born . . . God, it was a hundred years ago . . . ! Daddy would stop writing early, put on these galoshes and come looking for me, jingling the fasteners like castanets. It was a kind of mating call, almost . . . (*She jingles them.*) The Common was always deserted after a storm, we had the whole place to ourselves. It was so romantic . . . We'd haul the sled up Beacon Street, stop under the State House, and aim it straight down to the Park Street Church, which was much further away in those days . . . Then Daddy would lie down on the sled, I'd lower myself on top of him, we'd rock back and forth a few times to gain momentum and then . . . WHOOOOO OOOSSSSSSSSHHHHH . . . down we'd plunge like a pair of eagles locked in a spasm of love making. God, it was wonderful! . . . The city whizzing past us at 90 miles an hour . . . the cold . . . the darkness . . . Daddy's hair in my mouth . . . GAR . . . REMEMBER HOW WE USED TO GO SLEDDING IN THE OLD DAYS . . . ? Sometimes he'd lie on top of me. That was fun. I liked that even more. (*in her fog horn voice*) GARRRRRRRRRD-NERRRRR . . . ?

MAGS. Didn't he say he was going out this afternoon?

FANNY. Why, so he did! I completely forgot. (*She takes off the galoshes.*) I'm getting just as bad as him. (*She drops them into a different carton.*) Gar's galoshes, Cotuit. (*a pause*)

MAGS. (*picks up the table cloth again, holds it high over her head*) Isn't this fabulous . . . ? (*She then wraps FANNY in it.*) It's the perfect backdrop. Look what it does to your skin.

FANNY. Mags, what *are* you doing?

MAGS. It makes you glow like a pomegranate . . . (*She whips it off her.*) Now all I need is a hammer and nails . . . (*She finds them.*) YES! (*She climbs up the stepladder and starts hammering a corner of the cloth into the moulding of one of the windows.*) This is going to look so great . . . ! I've never seen such a color!

FANNY. Darling, what is going on . . . ?

MAGS. Rembrandt, eat your heart out! You 17th Century Dutch hasbeen, you. (*She hammers more furiously.*)

FANNY. MARGARET, THIS IS NOT A CONSTRUCTION SITE . . . PLEASE . . . STOP IT . . . YOO HOOOOO . . . DO YOU HEAR ME . . . ?

(*GARDNER suddenly appears, dressed in a raincoat.*)

FANNY. MARGARET, WILL YOU PLEASE STOP THAT RACKET?!

GARDNER. YES, DEAR, HERE I AM. I I JUST STEPPED OUT FOR A WALK DOWN CHESTNUT STREET. BEAUTIFUL AFTERNOON, ABSOLUTELY BEAUTIFUL!

FANNY. (*to MAGS*) YOU'RE GOING TO RUIN THE WALLS TO SAY NOTHING OF MAMA'S BEST TABLE CLOTH . . . MAGS, DO YOU HEAR ME? . . . YOO HOO . . . !

MAGS. (*Is done, she stops.*) There!

GARDNER. WHY THAT LOOKS VERY NICE, MAGS, very nice indeed . . .

FANNY. DARLING, I MUST INSIST you stop that dreadful . . .

MAGS. (*steps down, stands back and looks at it*) That's it. That's *IT!*

FANNY. (*to GARDNER, worried*) Where have you been?

(*MAGS kisses her fingers at the backdrop and settles back into her banana cake.*)

GARDNER. (*to FANNY*) You'll never guess who I ran into on Chestnut Street . . . Pate Baldwin! (*He takes his coat off and drops it on the floor. He then sits in one of the posing chairs MAGS has pulled over by the window.*)

MAGS. (*mouth full of cake*) Oh Daddy, I'm nowhere near ready for you yet.

FANNY. (*picks up his coat and hands it to him*) Darling, coats do *not* go on the floor.

GARDNER. (*rises, but forgets where he's supposed to go*) He was in terrible shape. I hardly recognized him. Well, it's the Parkinson's disease . . .

FANNY. You mean, Hodgkin's disease . . .

GARDNER. Hodgkin's disease . . . ?

MAGS. (*leaves her cake and returns to the table cloth*) Now to figure out exactly how to use this gorgeous light . . .

FANNY. Yes, Pate has Hodgkin's disease, not Parkinson's disease. Sammy Bishop has Parkinson's disease. In the closet . . . your coat goes . . . in the closet!

GARDNER. You're absolutely right! Pate has Hodgkin's disease. (*He stands motionless, the coat over his arm.*)

FANNY. . . . and Goat Davis has Addison's disease.

GARDNER. I always get them confused.

FANNY. (*pointing towards the closet*) That way . . . (*GARDNER exits to the closet; FANNY, calling after him.*) GRACE PHELPS HAS IT TOO, I THINK. Or, it might be Hodgkin's, like Pate. I can't remember.

GARDNER. (*returns with a hanger*) Doesn't the Goat have Parkinson's disease.

FANNY. No, that's Sammy Bishop.

GARDNER. God, I haven't seen the Goat in ages! (*The coat still over his arm, he hands FANNY the hanger.*)

FANNY. He hasn't been well.

GARDNER. Didn't Heppy . . . *die?!*

FANNY. What are you giving me this for? . . . Oh, Heppy's been dead for years. She died on the same day as Luster Bright, don't you remember?

GARDNER. I always liked her.

FANNY. (*gives him back the hanger*) Here, I don't want this.

GARDNER. She was awfully attractive.

FANNY. Who?

GARDNER. Heppy!

FANNY. Oh yes, Heppy had real charm.

MAGS. (*keeps experimenting with draping the table cloth*) Better . . . better . . .

GARDNER. . . . which is something the Goat is short on, if you ask me. He has Hodgkin's disease, doesn't he? (*puts his raincoat back on and sits down*)

FANNY. Darling, what *are* you doing? I thought you wanted to hang up your coat!

GARDNER. (*after a pause*) OH YES, THAT'S RIGHT! (*He goes back to the closet; a pause.*)

FANNY. Where were we?

GARDNER. (*returns with yet another hanger*) Let's see . . .

FANNY. (*takes both hangers from him*) FOR GOD'S SAKE, GAR, PAY ATTENTION!

GARDNER. It was something about the Goat . . .

FANNY. (*takes the coat from GARDNER*) HERE, LET ME DO IT . . . ! (*under her breath to MAGS*) See what I mean about him? You don't know the half of it! (*She hangs it up in the closet.*) Not the half.

MAGS. (*still tinkering with the backdrop*) Almost . . . almost . . .

GARDNER. (*sitting back down on one of the posing chairs*) Oh Fan, did I tell you, I ran into Pate Baldwin just now. I'm afraid he's not long for this world.

FANNY. (*returning*) Well, it's that Hodgkin's disease . . . (*She sits in the posing chair next to him.*)

GARDNER. God, I'd hate to see him go. He's one of the great editors of our times. I couldn't have done it without him. He gave me everything, everything!

MAGS. (*makes a final adjustment*) Yes, that's it! (*She stands back and gazes at them.*) You look wonderful . . . !

FANNY. Isn't it getting to be . . . (*She taps at an imaginary watch on her wrist and drains an imaginary glass.*) . . . *cocktail time?!*

GARDNER. (*looks at his watch*) On the button, on the button! (*He rises.*)

FANNY. I'll have the usual, please. Do join us, Mags! Daddy bought some Dubonnet especially for you!

MAGS. Hey. I was just getting some ideas.

GARDNER. (*To MAGS, as he exits for the bar.*) How about a little . . . *Dubonnet* to wet your whistle?

FANNY. Oh Mags, it's like old times having you back with us like this!

GARDNER. (*offstage*) THE USUAL FOR YOU, FAN?

FANNY. I wish we saw more of you . . . PLEASE! . . . Isn't he darling? Have you ever known anyone more darling than Daddy . . . ?

GARDNER. (*offstage; singing from the bar*) "You Made Me Love You",* etc. MAGS, HOW ABOUT YOU? . . . A LITTLE . . . DUBONNET . . . ?

FANNY. Oh, *do* join us!   MAGS. (*to GARDNER*)
                                 No, nothing, thanks!

FANNY. Well, what do you think of your aged parents picking up and moving to Cotuit year round? Pretty crazy, eh what? . . . Just the gulls, oysters and us!

GARDNER. (*returns with FANNY's drink*) Here you go . . .

FANNY. Why thank you, Gar. (*to MAGS*) You sure you won't join us?

GARDNER. (*lifts his glass towards FANNY and*

---

*Note: This song is still under copyright protection. Permission to use it in productions of *Painting Churches* ought to be procured from the copyright owner.

MAGS) Cheers! (*GARDNER and FANNY take that first life-saving gulp.*)

FANNY. Aaaaahhhhh!   GARDNER. Hits the spot, hits the spot!

MAGS. Well, I certainly can't do you like that!

FANNY. Why not? I think we look very . . . *comme il faut!* (*She slouches into a rummy pose, GARDNER joins her.*) WAIT . . . I'VE GOT IT! I'VE GOT IT! (*She whispers excitedly to GARDNER.*)

MAGS. Come on, let's not start this again!

GARDNER. What's that? . . . Oh yes . . . yes, yes . . . I know the one you mean. Yes, right, right . . . of course. (*a pause*)

FANNY. How's . . . *this* . . . ?! (*FANNY grabs a large serving fork and they fly into an imitation of Grant Wood's "American Gothic."*)

MAGS. . . . and I wonder why it's taken me all these years to get you to pose for me. You just don't take me seriously! Poor old Mags and her ridiculous portraits . . .

FANNY. Oh darling, your portraits aren't *ridiculous!* They may not be all that one *hopes* for, but they're certainly not . . .

MAGS. Remember how you behaved at my first group show in Soho? . . . Oh, come on, you remember. It was a real circus! Think back . . . It was about six years ago . . . Daddy had just been awarded some presidential medal of achievement and you insisted he wear it around his neck on a bright red ribbon, and you wore this . . . *huge* feathered hat to match! I'll never forget it! It was the size of a giant pizza with 20 inch red turkey feathers shooting straight up into the air . . . Oh come on, you remember, don't you . . . ?

FANNY. (*leaping to her feet*) HOLD EVERYTHING! THIS IS IT! THIS IS REALLY IT! Forgive me for interrupting, Mags darling, it'll just take a minute. (*She whispers excitedly to GARDNER.*)

MAGS. I had about eight portraits in the show, mostly of friends of mine, except for this old one I'd done of Mrs. Crowninshield.

GARDNER. All right, all right . . . let's give it a whirl. (*A pause, then they mime Michelangelo's "Pieta" with GARDNER lying across FANNY's lap as the dead Christ.*)

MAGS. (*depressed*) "The Pieta." Terrific!

FANNY. (*jabbing GARDNER in the ribs*) Hey, we're getting good at this.

GARDNER. Of course it would help if we didn't have all these modern clothes on.

MAGS. AS I WAS SAYING . . .

FANNY. Sorry, Mags . . . sorry . . . (*Huffing and creaking with the physical exertion of it all, they return to their seats.*)

MAGS. . . . As soon as you stepped foot in the gallery you spotted it and cried out, "MY GOD, WHAT'S MILLICENT CROWNINSHIELD DOING HERE?" Everyone looked up what with Daddy's clanking medal and your amazing hat which I was sure would take off and start flying around the room. A crowd gathered . . . Through some utter fluke, you latched on to *the* most important critic in the city, I mean . . . Mr. Modern Art himself, and you hauled him over to the painting, trumpeting out for all to hear, "THAT'S MILLICENT CROWNINSHIELD! I GREW UP WITH HER. SHE LIVES RIGHT DOWN THE STREET FROM US IN BOSTON. BUT IT'S A VERY POOR LIKENESS, IF YOU ASK ME! HER NOSE ISN'T NEARLY THAT LARGE AND SHE DOESN'T HAVE SOMETHING QUEER GROWING OUT OF HER CHIN! THE CROWNINSHIELDS ARE REALLY QUITE GOOD

LOOKING, STUFFY, BUT GOOD LOOKING NONE-THELESS!"

GARDNER. (*suddenly jumps up, ablaze*) WAIT, WAIT . . . IF IT'S MICHELANGELO YOU WANT . . . I'm sorry, Mags . . . One more . . . just one more . . . please?

MAGS. Sure, why not? Be my guest.

GARDNER. *Fanny, prepare yourself!* (*He whispers into her ear.*)

FANNY. THE BEST! . . . IT'S THE BEST! OH MY DEAREST, YOU'RE A GENIUS, AN ABSOLUTE GENIUS! (*more whispering*) But I think *you* should be God.

GARDNER. Me? . . . Really?

FANNY. Yes, it's much more appropriate.

GARDNER. Well, if you say so . . .

(*FANNY and GARDNER ease down to the floor with some difficulty and lie on their sides, FANNY as Adam, GARDNER as God, their fingers inching closer and closer in the attitude of Michelangelo's "The Creation." Finally, they touch.*)

MAGS. (*cheers, whistles, applauds*) THREE CHEERS . . . VERY GOOD . . . NICELY DONE, NICELY DONE! (*They hold the pose a moment more, flushed with pleasure, then rise, dust themselves off and grope back to their chairs.*) So, there we were . . .

FANNY. Yes, *do* go on . . . !

MAGS. . . . huddled around Millicent Crowninshield, when you whipped into your pocketbook and suddenly announced, "HOLD EVERYTHING! I'VE GOT A PHOTOGRAPH OF HER RIGHT HERE, THEN YOU CAN SEE WHAT SHE REALLY LOOKS LIKE!" . . . You then proceeded to crouch down to the

floor and dump everything out of your bag, and I mean
. . . *everything!* . . . Leaking packets of sequins and
gummed stars, sea shells, odd pieces of fur, crochet
hooks, a Monarch butterfly embedded in plastic, dental
floss, antique glass buttons, small jingling bells, lace
. . . I thought I'd die! Just sink to the floor and quietly
die! . . . You couldn't find it, you see. I mean, you
spent the rest of the afternoon on your hands and knees
crawling through this ocean of junk muttering, "It's *got*
to be here somewhere, I know I had it with me!"
. . . Then Daddy pulled me into the thick of it all and
said, "By the way, have you met our daughter Mags yet?
She's the one who did all these pictures . . . paintings
. . . portraits . . . whatever you call them." (*She drops
to her hands and knees and begins crawling out of the
room.*) By this time, Mum had somehow crawled out of
the gallery and was lost on another floor. She began
calling for me . . . "YOO HOO, MAGS . . . WHERE
ARE YOU? . . . OH MÁGS, DARLING . . .
HELLO . . . ? ARE YOU THERE . . . ?" (*She re-
enters and faces them.*) This was at my *first* show.

BLACKOUT

SCENE 3

*Twenty-four hours later. The impact of the impending
move has struck with hurricane force. FANNY has
lugged all their clothing into the room and dumped
it in various cartons. There are coats, jackets, shoes,
skirts, suits, hats, sweaters, dresses, the works. She
and GARDNER are seated on the sofa, going
through it all.*

FANNY. (*wearing a different hat and dress, holds up a ratty overcoat*) What about this gruesome old thing?

GARDNER. (*Is wearing several sweaters and vests, a Hawaiian holiday shirt, and a variety of scarves and ties around his neck. He holds up a pair of shoes.*) God . . . remember these shoes? Pound gave them to me when he came back from Italy. I remember it vividly.

FANNY. *Do* let me give it to the Thrift Shop! (*She stuffs the coat into the appropriate carton.*)

GARDNER. He bought them for me in Rome. Said he couldn't resist, bought himself a pair too since we both wore the same size. God, I miss him! (*pause*) HEY, WHAT ARE YOU DOING WITH MY OVERCOAT?!

FANNY. Darling, it's threadbare!

GARDNER. But that's my overcoat! (*He grabs it out of the carton.*) I've been wearing it every day for the past 35 years!

FANNY. That's just my point: it's had it.

GARDNER. (*puts it on over everything else*) There's nothing wrong with this coat!

FANNY. I trust you remember that the cottage is an eighth the size of this place and you simply won't have room for half this stuff! (*She holds up a sports jacket.*) This dreary old jacket, for instance. You've had it since Hector was a pup!

GARDNER. (*grabs it and puts it on over his coat*) Oh no you don't . . .

FANNY. . . . and this God-awful hat . . .

GARDNER. Let me see that. (*He stands next to her and they fall into a lovely frieze.*)

MAGS. (*suddenly pops out from behind a wardrobe carton with a flash camera and takes a picture of them*) PERFECT!

| FANNY. (*hands flying to her face*) GOOD | GARDNER. (*hands flying to his heart*) |

GOD, WHAT   JESUS CHRIST, I'VE
WAS THAT . . . ?   BEEN SHOT!

MAGS. (*walks to the* C. *of the room, advancing the film*) That was terrific. See if you can do it again.

FANNY. What *are* you doing . . . ?

GARDNER. (*feeling his chest*) Is there blood?

FANNY. I see lace everywhere . . .

MAGS. It's all right, I was just taking a picture of you. I often use a Polaroid at this stage.

FANNY. (*rubbing her eyes*) Really Mags, you might have given us some warning!

MAGS. But that's the whole point: to catch you unawares!

GARDNER. (*rubbing his eyes*) It's the damndest thing . . . I see lace everywhere.

FANNY. Yes, so do I . . .

GARDNER. It's rather nice, actually. It looks as if you're wearing a veil.

FANNY. I *am* wearing a veil! (*The camera spits out the photograph.*)

MAGS. OH GOODY, HERE COMES THE PICTURE!

FANNY. (*grabs the partially developed print out of her hands*) Let me see, let me see . . .

GARDNER. Yes, let's have a look.(*They have another quiet moment together looking at the photograph.*)

MAGS. (*tip toes away from them and takes another picture*) YES!

FANNY. NOT AGAIN!   GARDNER. WHAT
PLEASE, DARLING!   WAS THAT . . . ?
                          WHAT
                          HAPPENED . . . ?

(*They stagger towards each other.*)

MAGS. I'm sorry, I just couldn't resist. You looked so . . .

FANNY. WHAT ARE YOU TRYING TO DO . . . *BLIND* US?!

GARDNER. Really, Mags, enough is enough . . . (*GARDNER and FANNY keep stumbling about, kiddingly.*)

FANNY. Are you still there, Gar?

GARDNER. Right as rain, right as rain!

MAGS. I'm sorry, I didn't mean to scare you. It's just a photograph can show you things you weren't aware of. Here, have a look. (*She gives them to FANNY.*) Well, I'm going out to the kitchen to get something to eat. Anybody want anything? (*She exits.*)

FANNY. (*looking at the photos, half amused, half horrified*) Oh, Gardner, have you ever . . . ?

GARDNER. (*looks at them and laughs*) Good grief . . .

MAGS. (*offstage from the kitchen*) IS IT ALL RIGHT IF I TAKE THE REST OF THIS TAPIOCA FROM LAST NIGHT?

FANNY. IT'S ALL RIGHT WITH ME. How about you, Gar?

GARDNER. Sure, go right ahead. I've never been that crazy about tapioca.

FANNY. What are you talking about, tapioca is one of your favorites.

MAGS. (*enters, slurping from a large bowl*) Mmmm-mmmm . . .

FANNY. Really, Mags, I've never seen anyone eat as much as you.

MAGS. (*takes the photos back*) It's strange. I only do this when I come home.

FANNY. What's the matter, don't I feed you enough?

GARDNER. Gee, it's hot in here! (*starts taking off his coat*)

FANNY. God knows, you didn't eat anything as a child! I've never seen such a fussy eater. Gar, what *are* you doing?

GARDNER. Taking off some of these clothes. It's hotter than Tofit in here! (*shedding clothes to the floor*)

MAGS. (*looking at her photos*) Yes, I like you looking at each other like that . . .

FANNY. (*to GARDNER*) Please watch where you're dropping things, I'm trying to keep some order around here.

GARDNER. (*picks up what he dropped, dropping even more in the process*) Right, right . . .

MAGS. Now all I've got to do is figure out what you should wear.

FANNY. Well, I'm going to wear my long black dress, and you'd be a fool not to do Daddy in his tuxedo. He looks so distinguished in it, just like a banker!

MAGS. I haven't really decided yet.

FANNY. Just because you walk around looking like something the cat dragged in, doesn't mean Daddy and I want to, do we, Gar? (*GARDNER is making a worse and worse tangle of his clothes.*) HELLO . . . ?

GARDNER. (*looks up at FANNY*) Oh yes, awfully attractive, awfully attractive!

FANNY. (*to MAGS*) If you don't mind me saying so, I've never seen you looking so forlorn. You'll never catch a husband looking that way. Those peculiar clothes, that God-awful hair . . . Really, Mags, it's very distressing!

MAGS. I don't think my hair's so bad, not that it's terrific or anything . . .

FANNY. Well, I don't see other girls walking around like you. I mean, girls from your background. What would Lyman Wigglesworth think if he saw you in the street?

MAGS. Lyman Wigglesworth?! . . . Uuuuuuughhh-hhhh! (*She shudders.*)

FANNY. Alright then, that brilliant Cabot boy . . . what *is* his name?

GARDNER. Sammy.

FANNY. No, not Sammy . . .

GARDNER. Stephen.

FANNY. Oh, for God's sake, Gardner . . .

GARDNER. Stephen . . . Stanley . . . Stuart . . . Sheldon . . . Sherlock . . . Sherlock. It's Sherlock!

MAGS. Spence!

FANNY. SPENCE, THAT'S IT! HIS NAME IS SPENCE!

GARDNER. THAT'S IT . . . SPENCE! SPENCE CABOT!

FANNY. Spence Cabot was first in his class at Harvard.

MAGS. Mum, he has no facial hair.

FANNY. He has his own law firm on Arlington Street.

MAGS. Spence Cabot has six fingers on his right hand!

FANNY. So, he isn't the best looking thing in the world. Looks isn't everything. He can't help it if he has extra fingers. Have a little sympathy!

MAGS. But the extra one has this weird nail on it that looks like a talon . . . it's long and black and (*She shudders.*)

FANNY. No one's perfect, darling. He has lovely handwriting and an absolutely saintly mother. Also, he's as rich as Croesus! He's alot more promising than some of those creatures you've dragged home. What was the name of that dreadful Frenchman who smelled like sweaty socks? . . . Jean Duke of Scripto?

MAGS. (*laughing*) Jean-Luc Zichot!

FANNY. . . . and that peculiar little Oriental fellow with all the teeth! Really, Mags, he could have been put on display at the circus!

MAGS. Oh yes, Tsu Chin. He was strange, but very sexy . . .

FANNY. (*shudders*) He had such tiny . . . feet! Really, Mags, you've got to bear down. You're not getting any younger. Before you know it, all the nice young men will be taken and then where will you be? . . . All by yourself in that grim little apartment of yours with those peculiar clothes and that bright red hair . . .

MAGS. MY HAIR IS NOT BRIGHT RED!

FANNY. I only want what's best for you, you know that. You seem to go out of your way to look wanting. I don't understand it . . . Gar, what *are* you putting your coat on for? . . . You look like some derelict out on the street. We don't wear coats in the house. (*She helps him out of it.*) That's the way . . . I'll just put this in the carton along with everything else . . . (*She drops it into the carton, then pauses.*) Isn't it about time for . . . *cocktails!*

GARDNER. What's that? (*FANNY taps her wrist and mimes drinking. GARDNER looks at his watch.*) Right you are, right you are! (*exits to the bar*) THE USUAL . . . ?

FANNY. *Please!*

GARDNER. (*offstage*) HOW ABOUT SOMETHING FOR YOU, MAGS?

MAGS. SURE WHY NOT . . . ? LET 'ER RIP!

GARDNER. (*offstage*) WHAT'S THAT . . . ?

FANNY. SHE SAID   MAGS. I'LL HAVE
YES. SHE SAID YES!   SOME DUBONNET!

GARDNER. (*poking his head back in*) How about a little Dubonnet?

FANNY. That's just what she said . . . she'd like some . . . Dubonnet!

GARDNER. (*goes back to the bar and sings a Jolson tune*) GEE, IT'S GREAT HAVING YOU BACK LIKE

THIS, MAGS . . . IT'S JUST GREAT! (*more singing*)

FANNY. (*leaning closer to MAGS*) You have such *potential,* darling! It breaks my heart to see how you've let yourself go. If Lyman Wigglesworth . . .

MAGS. Amazing as it may seem, I don't *care* about Lyman Wigglesworth!

FANNY. From what I've heard, he's quite a lady killer!

MAGS. But with whom? . . . Don't think I haven't heard about his fling with . . . Hopie Stonewall!

FANNY. (*begins to laugh*) Oh God, let's not get started on Hopie Stonewall again . . . ten feet tall with spots on her neck . . . (*to GARDNER*) OH DARLING, DO HURRY BACK! WE'RE TALKING ABOUT PATHETIC HOPIE STONEWALL!

MAGS. It's not so much her incredible height and spotted skin, it's those tiny pointed teeth and the size 11 shoes!

FANNY. I love it when you're like this!

(*MAGS starts clomping around the room making tiny pointed teeth nibbling sounds.*)

FANNY. GARDNER . . . YOU'RE MISSING EVERYTHING! (*still laughing*) Why is it Boston girls are always so . . . tall?

MAGS. Hopie Stonewall isn't a Boston girl, she's a giraffe. (*She prances around the room with an imaginary dwarf-sized Lyman.*) She's perfect for Lyman Wigglesworth!

GARDNER. (*returns with FANNY's drink which he hands her*) Now, where were we . . . ?

FANNY. (*trying not to laugh*) HOPIE STONEWALL! . . .

GARDNER. Oh yes, she's the very tall one, isn't she? (*FANNY and MAGS burst out laughing.*)

MAGS. The only hope for us . . . "Boston girls" is to get as far away from our kind as possible.

FANNY. She always asks after you, darling. She's very fond of you, you know.

MAGS. Please, I don't want to hear!

FANNY. Your old friends are *always* asking after you.

MAGS. It's not so much how creepy they all are, as how much they remind me of myself!

FANNY. But you're not "creepy," darling . . . just . . . shabby!

MAGS. I mean, give me a few more inches and some brown splotches here and there, and Hopie and I could be sisters!

FANNY. (*in a whisper to GARDNER*) Don't you love it when Mags is like this? I could listen to her forever!

MAGS. I mean . . . look at me!

FANNY. (*gasping*) Don't stop, don't stop!

MAGS. Awkward . . . plain . . . I don't know how to dress, I don't know how to talk. When people find out Daddy's my father, they're always amazed . . . "Gardner Church is YOUR father?! Aw come on, you're kidding?!"

FANNY. (*in a whisper*) Isn't she divine . . . ?

MAGS. Sometimes I don't even tell them. I pretend I grew up in the midwest somewhere . . . farming people . . . we work with our hands.

GARDNER. (*to MAGS*) Well, how about a little refill . . . ?

MAGS. No, no more thanks. (*pause*)

FANNY. What did you have to go and interrupt her for? She was just getting up a head of steam . . . ?

MAGS. (*walking over to her easel*) The great thing about being a portrait painter you see is, it's the *other* guy that's exposed, you're safely hidden behind the canvas and easel. (*standing behind it*) You can be as plain as a pitchfork, as inarticulate as mud, but it doesn't matter because you're completely concealed: your body, your face, your intentions. Just as you make your most intimate move, throw open your soul . . . they stretch and yawn, remembering the dog has to be let out at five . . . To be so invisible while so enthralled . . . it takes your breath away!

GARDNER. Well put, Mags. Awfully well put!

MAGS. That's why I've always wanted to paint you, to see if I'm up to it. It's quite a risk. Remember what I went through as a child with my great master-piece . . . ?

FANNY. You painted a masterpiece when you were a child . . . ?

MAGS. Well, it was a masterpiece to me.

FANNY. I had no idea you were precocious as a child. Gardner, do you remember Mags painting a masterpiece as a child?

MAGS. I didn't paint it. It was something I made!

FANNY. Well, this is all news to me! Gar, *do* get me another drink! I haven't had this much fun in years! (*She hands him her glass and reaches for MAGS'.*) Come on, darling, join me . . .

MAGS. No, no more, thanks. I don't really like the taste.

FANNY. Oh come on, kick up your heels for once!

MAGS. No, nothing . . . really.

FANNY. Please? Pretty please . . . ? To keep me company?!

MAGS. (*hands GARDNER her glass*) Oh, all right, what the hell . . .

FANNY. That's a good girl!

GARDNER. (*exiting*) Coming right up, coming right up!

FANNY. (*yelling after him*) DON'T GIVE ME TOO

MUCH NOW. THE LAST ONE WAS AWFULLY STRONG . . . AND HURRY BACK SO YOU DON'T MISS ANYTHING . . . ! Daddy's so cunning, I don't know what I'd do without him. If anything should happen to him, I'd just . . .

MAGS. Mummy, nothing's going to happen to him . . . !

FANNY. Well, wait 'til you're our age, it's no garden party. Now . . . where were we . . . ?

MAGS. My first masterpiece . . .

FANNY. Oh yes, but *do* wait til Daddy gets back so he can hear it too . . . YOO HOOOO . . . GARRRRRRD-NERRRRRR? . . . ARE YOU COMING . . . ? (*silence*) Go and check on him, will you?

GARDNER. (*Enters with both drinks; he's shaken.*) I couldn't find the ice.

FANNY. Well, *finally!*

GARDNER. It just up and disappeared . . . (*hands FANNY her drink*) There you go. (*FANNY kisses her fingers and takes a hefty swig.*) Mags. (*hands her hers*)

MAGS. Thanks, Daddy.

GARDNER. Sorry about the ice.

MAGS. No problem, no problem. (*GARDNER sits down; silence.*)

FANNY. (*to MAGS*) Well, drink up, drink up! (*MAGS downs it in one gulp.*) GOOD GIRL! . . . Now, what's all this about a masterpiece . . . ?

MAGS. I did it during that winter you sent me away from the dinner table. I was about nine years old.

FANNY. We sent you from the dinner table?

MAGS. I was banished for six months.

FANNY. You *were* . . . ? How extraordinary!

MAGS. Yes, it *was* rather extraordinary!

FANNY. But why?

MAGS. Because I played with my food.

FANNY. You did?

MAGS. I used to squirt it out between my front teeth.

FANNY. Oh, I remember that! God, it used to drive me crazy, absolutely . . . crazy! (*pause*) "MARGARET, STOP THAT OOZING RIGHT THIS MINUTE, YOU ARE *NOT* A TUBE OF TOOTHPASTE!"

GARDNER. Oh yes . . .

FANNY. It was perfectly disgusting!

GARDNER. I remember. She used to lean over her plate and squirt it out in long runny ribbons . . .

FANNY. That's enough, dear.

GARDNER. They were quite colorful, actually; decorative almost. She made the most intricate designs. They looked rather like small, moist Oriental rugs . . .

FANNY. (*to MAGS*) But why, darling? What on earth possessed you to do it?

MAGS. I couldn't swallow anything. My throat just closed up. I don't know, I must have been afraid of choking or something.

GARDNER. I remember one in particular. We'd had chicken fricassee and spinach . . . She made the most extraordinary . . .

FANNY. (*to GARDNER*) WILL YOU PLEASE SHUT UP?! (*pause*) Mags, what *are* you talking about? You never choked in your entire life! This is the most distressing conversation I've ever had. Don't you think it's distressing, Gar?

GARDNER. Well, that's not quite the word I'd use.

FANNY. What word *would* you use, then?

GARDNER. I don't know right off the bat, I'd have to think about it.

FANNY. THEN, THINK ABOUT IT! (*silence*)

MAGS. I guess I was afraid of making a mess. I don't know, you were awfully strict about table manners. I was always afraid of losing control. What if I started to choke and began spitting up over everything . . . ?

FANNY. Alright, dear, that's enough.

MAGS. No, I was really terrified about making a mess, you always got so mad whenever I spilled. If I just got rid of everything in neat little curly-cues beforehand, you see . . .

FANNY. I SAID: THAT'S ENOUGH! (*silence*)

MAGS. *I* thought it was quite ingenious, but you didn't see it that way. You finally sent me from the table with, "When you're ready to eat like a human being, you can come back and join us!" . . . So, it was off to my room with a tray. But I couldn't seem to eat there either. I mean, it was so strange settling down to dinner in my *bedroom* . . . So I just flushed everything down the toilet and sat on my bed listening to you: clinkity clink, clatter clatter, slurp slurp . . . but that got pretty boring after awhile, so I looked around for something to do. It was wintertime because I noticed I'd left some crayons on top of my radiator and they'd melted down into these beautiful shimmering globs, like spilled jello, trembling and pulsing . . .

GARDNER. (*eyes closed*) "This luscious and impeccable fruit of life
Falls, it appears, of its own weight to earth . . ."

MAGS. Naturally, I wanted to try it myself, so I grabbed a red one and pressed it down against the hissing lid. It oozed and bubbled like raspberry jam!

GARDNER. "When you were Eve, its acrid juice was sweet,
Untasted, in its heavenly, orchard air . . ."

MAGS. I mean, that radiator was really hot! It took incredible will power not to let go, but I held on, whispering, "Mags, if you let go of this crayon, you'll be run

over by a truck on Newberry Street, so help you God!"
. . . So I pressed down harder, my fingers steaming and
blistering . . .

FANNY. I had no idea about any of this, did you, Gar?

MAGS. Once I'd melted one, I was hooked! I finished
off my entire supply in one night, mixing color over
color until my head swam . . . ! The heat, the smell, the
brilliance that sank and rose . . . I'd never felt such ex-
hiliaration! . . . Every week I spent my allowance on
crayons. I must have cleared out every box of Crayolas
in the city!

GARDNER. (*gazing at MAGS*) You know, I don't
think I've ever seen you looking prettier! You're awfully
attractive when you get going!

FANNY. Why, what a lovely thing to say.

MAGS. AFTER THREE MONTHS THAT RADIA-
TOR WAS . . . SPECTACULAR! I MEAN, IT
LOOKED LIKE SOME COLOSSAL FRUIT CAKE,
FIVE FEET TALL . . . !

FANNY. It sounds perfectly hideous.

MAGS. It was a knockout; shimmering with pinks and
blues, lavenders and maroons, turquoise and golds,
oranges and creams . . . For every color, I imagined a
taste . . . YELLOW: lemon curls dipped in sugar . . .
RED: glazed cherries laced with rum . . . GREEN: tiny
peppermint leaves veined with chocolate . . . PUR-
PLE: . . .

FANNY. That's quite enough!

MAGS. And then the frosting . . . ahhhh, the frosting! A satiny mix of white and silver . . . I kept it hidden under blankets during the day . . . My huge . . .
(*She starts laughing.*) . . . looming . . . teetering
sweet . . .

FANNY. I ASKED YOU TO STOP! GARDNER,
WILL YOU PLEASE GET HER TO STOP!

GARDNER. See here, Mags, Mum asked you to . . .

MAGS. I was so . . . *hungry* . . . losing weight every week. I looked like a scarecrow what with the bags under my eyes and bits of crayon wrapper leaking out of my clothes. It's a wonder you didn't notice. But finally you came to my rescue . . . If you could call what happened a rescue. It was more like a rout!

FANNY. Darling . . . *please!*   GARDNER. Now look, young lady . . .

MAGS. The winter was almost over . . . It was very late at night . . . I must have been having a nightmare because suddenly you and Daddy were at my bed, shaking me . . . I quickly glanced towards the radiator to see if it was covered . . . *It wasn't!* It glittered and towered in the moonlight like some . . . gigantic Viennese pastry! You followed my gaze and saw it. Mummy screamed . . . "WHAT HAVE YOU GOT IN HERE? . . . MAGS, WHAT HAVE YOU BEEN DOING?" . . . She crept forward and touched it, and then jumped back. "IT'S FOOD!" she cried . . . "IT'S ALL THE FOOD SHE'S BEEN SPITTING OUT! OH, GARDNER, IT'S A MOUNTAIN OF ROTTING GARBAGE!"

FANNY. (*softly*) Yes . . . it's coming back . . . it's coming back . . .

MAGS. Daddy exited as usual, left the premises. He fainted, just keeled over onto the floor . . .

GARDNER. Gosh, I don't remember any of this . . .

MAGS. My heart stopped! I mean, I knew it was all over. My lovely creation didn't have a chance. Sure enough . . . Out came the blow torch. Well, it couldn't have *really* been a blow torch, I mean, where would you have ever gotten a blow torch . . . ? I just have this very strong memory of you standing over my bed, your hair streaming around your face, aiming this . . . flame

thrower at my confection . . . my cake . . . my tart
. . . my strudel . . . "IT'S GOT TO BE DESTROYED
IMMEDIATELY! THE THING'S ALIVE WITH
VERMIN! . . . JUST LOOK AT IT! . . . IT'S PRAC-
TICALLY CRAWLING ACROSS THE ROOM!"
. . . Of course in a sense you were right. It *was* a monu-
ment of my cast-off dinners, only I hadn't built it with
food . . . I found my own materials. I was languishing
with hunger, but oh, dear Mother . . . I FOUND MY
OWN MATERIALS . . . !

FANNY. Darling . . . *please?!*

MAGS. I tried to stop you, but you wouldn't listen . . .
OUT SHOT THE FLAME! . . . I remember these
waves of wax rolling across the room and Daddy coming to, wondering what on earth was going on . . .
Well, what did you know about my abilities . . . ? You
see, I had . . . I mean, I *have* abilities . . . (*struggling
to say it*) I have abilities. I have . . . strong abilities. I
have . . . very strong abilities. They are very strong . . .
very very strong . . . (*She rises and runs out of the
room overcome as FANNY and GARDNER watch,
speechless.*)

THE CURTAIN FALLS

ACT TWO

SCENE 1

Three days later. Miracles have been accomplished. Almost all of the Church's furniture has been moved out and the cartons of dishes and clothing are gone. All that remains are odds and ends. MAGS' tableau looms, impregnable. FANNY and GARDNER are dressed in their formal evening clothes, frozen in their pose. They hold absolutely still. MAGS stands at her easel, her hands covering her eyes.

FANNY. All right, you can look now.

MAGS. (*removes her hands*) Yes . . . ! I told you you could trust me on the pose.

FANNY. Well, thank God you let us dress up. It makes all the difference. Now we really look like something.

MAGS. (*starts to sketch them*) I'll say . . . (*A silence as she sketches.*)

GARDNER. (*Recites Yeats' "The Song of Wandering Aengus" in a wonderfully resonant voice as they pose.*)
"I went out to the hazel wood,
Because a fire was in my head,
And cut and peeled a hazel wand,
And hooked a berry to a thread,
And when white moths were on the wing,
And moth-like stars were flickering out,
I dropped the berry in a stream
And caught a little silver trout.

When I had laid it on the floor
I went to blow the fire a-flame,
But something rustled on the floor,

55

And someone called me by my name:
It had become a glimmering girl
With apple blossoms in her hair
Who called me by my name and ran
And faded through the brightening air.

Though I am old with wandering
Through hollow lands and hilly lands,
I will find out where she has gone,
And kiss her lips and take her hands;
And walk among long dappled grass,
And pluck till time and times are done,
The silver apples of the moon,
The golden apples of the sun."
(*silence*)

FANNY. That's lovely, dear. Just lovely. Is it one of yours?

GARDNER. No, no, it's Yeats. I'm using it in my book.

FANNY. Well, you recited it beautifully, but then you've always recited beautifully. That's how you wooed me, in case you've forgotten . . . You must have memorized every love poem in the English language! There was no stopping you when you got going . . . your Shakespeare, Byron, and Shelley . . . you were shameless . . . *shameless!*

GARDNER. (*eyes closed*)
"I will find out where she has gone,
And kiss her lips and take her hands . . ."

FANNY. And then there was your own poetry to do battle with; your sonnets and quatrains. When you got going with them, there was nothing left of me! You could have had your pick of any girl in Boston! Why you chose me, I'll never understand. I had no looks to speak of and nothing much in the brains department

. . . Well, what did you know about women and the world . . . ? What did any of us know . . . ? (*silence*) GOD, MAGS, HOW LONG ARE WE SUPPOSED TO SIT LIKE THIS . . . ? IT'S AGONY!

MAGS. (*working away*) You're doing fine . . . just fine . . .

FANNY. (*breaking her pose*) It's so . . . boring!

MAGS. Come on, don't move. You can have a break soon.

FANNY. I had no idea it would be so boring!

GARDNER. Gee, I'm enjoying it.

FANNY. You *would* . . . ! (*a pause*)

GARDNER. (*begins reciting more Yeats, almost singing it*)

"He stood among a crowd at Drumahair;

His heart hung all upon a silken dress,

And he had known at last some tenderness,

Before earth made of him her sleepy care;

But when a man poured fish into a pile,

It seemed they raised their little silver heads . . ."

FANNY. Gar . . . PLEASE! (*She lurches out of her seat.*) God, I can't take this anymore!

MAGS. (*keeps sketching GARDNER*) I know it's tedious as first, but it gets easier . . .

FANNY. It's like a Chinese water torture ! . . . (*crosses to MAGS and looks at GARDNER posing*) Oh darling, you look marvelous, absolutely marvelous! Why don't you just do Daddy!?

MAGS. Because you look marvelous too. I want to do you both!

FANNY. Please . . . ! I have one foot in the grave and you know it! Also, we're way behind in our packing. There's still one room left which everyone seems to have forgotten about!

GARDNER. Which one is that?

FANNY. You know perfectly well which one it is!

GARDNER. I do . . . ?

FANNY. Yes, you do!

GARDNER. Well, it's news to me.

FANNY. I'll give you a hint. It's in . . . *that* direction. (*She points.*)

GARDNER. The dining room.

FANNY. No.

GARDNER. The bedroom.

FANNY. No.

GARDNER. Mags' room.

FANNY. No.

GARDNER. The kitchen.

FANNY. *Gar . . . ?!*

GARDNER. The guest room?

FANNY. Your God awful study!

GARDNER. Oh, shit!

FANNY. That's right, "oh shit!" It's books and papers up to the ceiling! If you ask me, we should just forget it's there and quietly tip toe away . . .

GARDNER. My study . . . !

FANNY. Let the new owners dispose of everything . . .

GARDNER. (*gets out of his posing chair*) Now, just one minute . . .

FANNY. You never look at half the stuff in there!

GARDNER. I don't want you touching those books! They're mine!

FANNY. Darling, we're moving to a cottage the size of a handkerchief! Where, pray tell, is there room for all your books?

GARDNER. I don't know. We'll just have to make room!

MAGS. (*sketching away*) RATS!

FANNY. I don't know what we're doing fooling around with Mags like this when there's still so much to do . . .

GARDNER. (*sits back down, overwhelmed*) My study . . . !

FANNY. You can stay with her if you'd like, but one of us has got to tackle those books! (*She exits to his study.*)

GARDNER. I'm not up to this.

MAGS. Oh good, you're staying!

GARDNER. There's a lifetime of work in there . . .

MAGS. Don't worry, I'll help. Mum and I will be able to pack everything up in no time.

GARDNER. God . . .

MAGS. It won't be so bad . . .

GARDNER. I'm just not up to it.

MAGS. We'll all pitch in . . .

(*GARDNER sighs, speechless. A silence as MAGS keeps sketching him. FANNY comes staggering in with an armload of books which she drops to the floor with a crash.*)

GARDNER. WHAT   MAGS. GOOD GRIEF!
WAS THAT . . . ?!

FANNY. (*sheepish*) Sorry, sorry . . . (*She exits for more.*)

GARDNER. I don't know if I can take this . . .

MAGS. Moving is awful . . . I know . . .

GARDNER. (*settling back into his pose*) Ever since Mum began tearing the house apart, I've been having these dreams . . . I'm a child again back at 16 Louisberg Square . . . and this stream of moving men is carrying furniture into our house . . . van after van of tables and chairs, sofas and loveseats, desks and bureaus . . . rugs, bathtubs, mirrors, chiming clocks, pianos, ice boxes, china cabinets . . . but what's amazing is that all of it is familiar . . . (*FANNY comes in with another load which she drops on the floor. She exits for more.*) No matter how many items appear, I've seen every one of them before. Since my mother is standing in the midst of it directing traffic, I ask her where it's all coming from, but she doesn't hear me because of the racket . . . so finally I just scream out . . . "WHERE IS ALL THIS FURNITURE COMING FROM?" . . . Just as a moving man is carrying Toots into the room, she looks at me and says, "Why, from the land of Skye!" . . . The next thing I know, *people* are being carried in along with it . . . (*FANNY enters with her next load, drops it and exits.*) . . . people I've never seen before are sitting around our dining room table. A group of foreigners is going through my books, chattering in a language I've never heard before. A man is playing a Chopin Polonaise on Aunt Alice's piano. Several children are taking baths in our tubs from Cotuit . . .

MAGS. It sounds marvelous.

GARDNER. Well, it isn't marvelous at all because all of these perfect strangers have taken over our things . . . (*FANNY enters, hurls down another load and exits.*)

MAGS. How odd . . .

GARDNER. Well, it *is* odd, but then something even odder happens . . .

MAGS. (*sketching away*) Tell me, tell me!

GARDNER. Well, our beds are carried in. They're all made up with sheets and everything, but instead of all these strange people in them, *we're* in them . . . !

MAGS. What's so odd about that . . . ?

GARDNER. Well, you and Mum are brought in, both sleeping like angels . . . Mum snoring away to beat the band . . .

MAGS. Yes . . . (*FANNY enters with another load, lets it fall.*)

GARDNER. But there's no one in mine. It's completely empty, never even been slept in! It's as if I were dead or had never even existed . . . (*FANNY exits.*) "HEY . . . WAIT UP!" I yell to the moving men . . . "THAT'S MY BED YOU'VE GOT THERE!" but they don't stop, they don't even acknowledge me . . . "HEY, COME BACK HERE . . . I WANT TO GET INTO MY BED!" I cry again and I start running after them . . . down the hall, through the dining room, past the library . . . Finally I catch up to them and hurl myself right into the center of the pillow. Just as I'm about to land, the bed suddenly vanishes and I go crashing down to the floor like some insect that's been hit by a fly swatter!

FANNY. (*staggers in with her final load, drops it with a crash and then collapses in her posing chair*) THAT'S IT FOR ME! I'M DEAD! (*silence*) Come on, Mags, how about you doing a little work around here.

MAGS. That's all I've been doing! This is the first free moment you've given me!

FANNY. You should see all the books in there . . . and papers! There are enough loose papers to sink a ship!

GARDNER. Why is it we're moving, again . . . ?

FANNY. Because life is getting too complicated here.

GARDNER. (*remembering*) Oh yes . . .

FANNY. And we can't afford it anymore.

GARDNER. That's right, that's right . . .

FANNY. We don't have the . . . *income* we used to!

GARDNER. Oh yes . . . *income!*

FANNY. (*assuming her pose again*) Of course we have our savings and various trust funds, but I wouldn't dream of touching those!

GARDNER. No, no, you must never dip into capital!

FANNY. I told Daddy I'd be perfectly happy to buy a gun and put a bullet through our heads so we could avoid all this, but he wouldn't hear of it!

MAGS. (*sketching away*) No, I shouldn't think so. (*pause*)

FANNY. I've always admired people who kill themselves when they get to our stage of life. Well, no one can touch my Uncle Edmond in that department . . .

MAGS. I know, I know . . .

FANNY. The day before his 70th birthday he climbed to the top of the Old North Church and hurled himself face down into Salem Street! They had to scrape him up with a spatula! God, he was a remarkable man . . . state senator, President of Harvard . . .

GARDNER. (*rises and wanders over to his books*) Well, I guess I'm going to have to do something about all of these . . .

FANNY. . . . Come on, Mags, help Daddy! Why don't you start bringing in his papers . . .

(*GARDNER sits on the floor, picks up a book and soon is engrossed in it. MAGS keeps sketching, oblivious. Silence.*)

FANNY. (*to MAGS*) Darling . . . ? HELLO . . . ? (*They both ignore her.*) God, you two are impossible! Just look at you . . . heads in the clouds! No one would ever know we've got to be out of here in two days. If it weren't for me, nothing would get done around here . . . (*She starts stacking GARDNER's books into piles.*) There! That's all the maroon ones!

GARDNER. (*looks up*) What do you mean, *maroon* ones . . . ?!

FANNY. All your books that are maroon are in *this*

pile . . . and your books that are green in *that* pile . . . !
I'm trying to bring some order into your life for once.
This will make unpacking so much easier.

GARDNER. But my dear Fanny, it's not the color of a
book that distinguishes it, but what's *inside* it!

FANNY. This will be a great help, you'll see. Now what
about this awful striped thing? (*She picks up a slim,
aged volume.*) Can't it go . . . ?

GARDNER. No!

FANNY. But it's as queer as Dick's hat band! There are
no others like it.

GARDNER. Open it and read. Go on . . . open it!

FANNY. We'll get nowhere at this rate.

GARDNER. I said . . . READ!

FANNY. Really, Gar, I . . .

GARDNER. Read the dedication!

FANNY. (*opens and reads*) "To Gardner Church, you
led the way. With gratitude and affection, Robert
Frost." (*She closes it and hands it to him.*)

GARDNER. It was published the same year as my
"Salem Gardens."

FANNY. (*picking up a very dirty book*) Well, what
about this dreadful thing? It's filthy. (*She blows off a
cloud of dust.*)

GARDNER. Please . . . *please?!*

FANNY. (*looking through it*) It's all in French.

GARDNER. (*snatching it away from her*) Andre Mal-
raux gave me that . . . !

FANNY. I'm just trying to help.

GARDNER. It's a first edition of Baudelaire's "Fleurs
du Mal."

FANNY. (*giving it back*) Well, pardon me for living!

GARDNER. Why do you have to drag everything in
here in the first place . . . ?

FANNY. Because there's no room in your study. You ought to see the mess in there! . . . WAKE UP, MAGS, ARE YOU GOING TO PITCH IN OR NOT . . . ?!

GARDNER. I'm not up to this.

FANNY. Well, you'd better be unless you want to be left behind!

MAGS. (*stops her sketching*) Alright, alright . . . I just hope you'll give me some more time later this evening.

FANNY. (*to MAGS*) Since you're young and in the best shape, why don't you bring in the books and I'll cope with the papers. (*She exits to the study.*)

GARDNER. Now just a minute . . .

FANNY. (*offstage*) WE NEED A STEAM SHOVEL FOR THIS!

MAGS. O.K., what do you want me to do?

GARDNER. Look, I don't want you messing around with my . . . (*FANNY enters with an armful of papers which she drops into an empty carton.*) HEY, WHAT'S GOING ON HERE . . . ?

FANNY. I'm packing up your papers. COME ON, MAGS, LET'S GET CRACKING! (*She exits for more papers.*)

GARDNER. (*plucks several papers out of the carton*) What is this . . . ?

MAGS. (*exits into his study*) GOOD LORD, WHAT HAVE YOU DONE IN HERE . . . ?!

GARDNER. (*reading*) This is my manuscript. (*FANNY enters with another batch which she tosses on top of the others.*) What *are* you doing . . . ?!

FANNY. Packing, darling . . . PACKING! (*She exits for more.*)

GARDNER. SEE HERE, YOU CAN'T MANHAN-DLE MY THINGS THIS WAY! (*MAGS enters, stag-*

gering under a load of books which she sets down on the floor.) I PACK MY MANUSCRIPT! I KNOW WHERE EVERYTHING IS!

FANNY. (*offstage*) IF IT WERE UP TO YOU, WE'D NEVER GET OUT OF HERE! WE'RE UNDER A TIME LIMIT, GARDNER. KITTY'S PICKING US UP IN TWO DAYS . . . TWO . . . DAYS! (*She enters with a larger batch of papers and heads for the carton.*)

GARDNER. (*grabbing FANNY's wrist*) NOW, HOLD IT . . . ! JUST . . . HOLD IT RIGHT THERE . . . !

FANNY. OOOOOWWWWWWWW!

GARDNER. I PACK MY THINGS . . . !

FANNY. LET GO, YOU'RE HURTING ME!

GARDNER. THAT'S MY MANUSCRIPT! GIVE IT TO ME!

FANNY. (*lifting the papers high over her head*) I'M IN CHARGE OF THIS MOVE, GARDNER! WE'VE GOT TO GET CRACKING!

GARDNER. I said . . . GIVE IT TO ME!

MAGS. Come on, Mum, let him have it. (*They struggle.*)

GARDNER. (*finally wrenches the pages from her*) LET . . . ME . . . HAVE IT . . . ! THAT'S MORE LIKE IT . . . !

FANNY. (*soft and weepy*) You see what he's like . . . ? I try and help with his packing and what does he do . . . ?

GARDNER. (*rescues the rest of his papers from the carton*) YOU DON'T JUST THROW EVERYTHING INTO A BOX LIKE A PILE OF GARBAGE! THIS IS A BOOK, FANNY. SOMETHING I'VE BEEN WORKING ON FOR TWO YEARS . . . ! (*trying to assemble his papers, but only making things worse, dropping them all over the place*) You show a little respect for my things . . . you don't just throw them around every which way . . . It's tricky trying to make sense of poetry, it's much easier to write the stuff . . . that is, if you've still got it in you . . .

MAGS. Here, let me help . . . (*taking some of the papers*)

GARDNER. Criticism is tough sledding. You can't just dash off a few images here, a few rhymes there . . .

MAGS. Do you have these pages numbered in any way?

FANNY. (*returning to her posing chair*) HA!

GARDNER. This is just the introduction.

MAGS. I don't see any numbers on these.

GARDNER. (*exiting to his study*) The important stuff is in my study . . .

FANNY. (*to MAGS*) You don't know the half of it . . . *Not the half . . .* !

GARDNER. (*offstage; thumping around*) HAVE YOU SEEN THOSE YEATS POEMS I JUST HAD . . . ?

MAGS. (*reading over several pages*) What is this . . . ? It doesn't make sense. It's just fragments . . . pieces of poems.

FANNY. That's it, honey! That's his book. His great critical study! Now that he can't write his own poetry, he's trying to explain other people's. The only problem is, he can't get beyond typing them out. The poor lamb doesn't have the stamina to get beyond the opening stanzas, let alone trying to make sense of them.

GARDNER. (*thundering back with more papers which keep falling*) GOD DAMNIT, FANNY, WHAT DID YOU DO IN THERE? I CAN'T FIND ANYTHING!

FANNY. I just took the papers that were on your desk.

GARDNER. Well, the entire beginning is gone. (*He exits.*)

FANNY. I'M TRYING TO HELP YOU, DARLING!

GARDNER. (*returns with another armload*) SEE THAT . . . ? NO SIGN OF CHAPTER ONE OR TWO . . . (*He flings it all down to the floor.*)

FANNY. Gardner . . . PLEASE?!

GARDNER. (*kicking through the mess*) I TURN MY BACK FOR ONE MINUTE AND WHAT HAPPENS . . . ? MY ENTIRE STUDY IS TORN APART! (*He exits.*)

MAGS. Oh Daddy . . . don't . . . please . . . Daddy . . . *please?!*

GARDNER. (*returns with a new batch of papers which he tosses up into the air*) THROWN OUT . . . ! THE BEST PART IS THROWN OUT! . . . LOST . . . (*He starts to exit again.*)

MAGS. (*reads one of the fragments to steady herself*) "I have known the inexorable sadness of pencils, Neat in their boxes, dolor of pad and paper-weight, All the misery of manila folders and mucilage . . ."

They're beautiful . . . just beautiful.

GARDNER. (*stops*) Hey, what's that you've got there?

FANNY. It's your manuscript, darling. You see, it's right where you left it.

GARDNER. (*to MAGS*) Read that again.

MAGS.
"I have known the inexorable sadness of pencils, Neat in their boxes, dolor of pad and paper-weight, All the misery of manila folders and mucilage . . ."

GARDNER. Well, well, what do you know . . .

FANNY. (*hands him several random papers*) You see . . . no one lost anything. Everything's here, still in tact.

GARDNER. (*reads*)
"I knew a woman, lovely in her bones,

When small birds sighed, she would sigh back at them;
Ah, when she moved, she moved more ways than one:
The shapes a bright container can contain! . . ."

FANNY. (*hands him another*) And . . .

GARDNER. Ah yes, Frost. . . . (*reads*)
"Some say the world will end in fire,
Some say ice.
From what I've tasted of desire
I hold with those who favor fire."

FANNY. (*under her breath to MAGS*) He can't give up
the words. It's the best he can do. (*handing him another*)
Here you go, here's more.

GARDNER.
"Farm boys wild to couple
With anything   with soft-wooded trees
With mounds of earth   mounds
Of pinestraw   will keep themselves off
Animals by legends of their own . . ."

MAGS. (*eyes shut*) Oh Daddy, I can't bear it . . . I . . .

FANNY. Of course no one will ever publish this.

GARDNER. Oh, here's a marvelous one. Listen to this!
"There came a Wind like a Bugle—
It quivered through the Grass
And a Green Chill upon the Heat
So ominous did pass
We barred the Windows and the Doors
As from an Emerald Ghost—

The Doom's electric Moccasin . . ."

SHIT, WHERE DID THE REST OF IT GO . . . ?

FANNY. Well, don't ask *me*.

GARDNER. It just stopped in mid air!

FANNY. Then go look for the original.

GARDNER. Good idea, good idea! (*He exits to his study.*)

FANNY. (*to MAGS*) He's incontinent now too. He wets his pants, in case you haven't noticed. (*She starts laughing.*) You're not laughing. Don't you think it's funny? Daddy needs diapers . . . I don't know about you, but I could use a drink! GAR . . . WILL YOU GET ME A SPLASH WHILE YOU'RE OUT THERE . . . ?

MAGS. STOP IT!

FANNY. It means we can't go out anymore. I mean, what would people say . . . ?

MAGS. Stop it. Just stop it.

FANNY. My poet laureate can't hold it in! (*She laughs harder.*)

MAGS. That's enough . . . STOP IT . . . Mummy . . . I beg of you . . . *please stop it!*

GARDNER. (*Enters with a book and indeed a large stain has blossomed on his trousers. He plucks it away from his leg.*) Here we go . . . I found it . . .

FANNY. (*pointing at it*) See that? See . . . ? He just did it again! (*goes off into a shower of laughter*)

MAGS. (*looks, turns away*) SHUT . . . UP . . . ! (*building to a howl*) WILL YOU PLEASE JUST . . . SHUT . . . UP!

FANNY. (*to GARDNER*) Hey, what about that drink?

GARDNER. Oh yes . . . sorry, sorry . . . (*He heads towards the bar.*)

FANNY. Never mind, I'll get it, I'll get it. (*She exits, convulsed. Silence.*)

GARDNER. Well, where were we . . . ?

MAGS. (*near tears*) Your poem.

GARDNER. Oh yes . . . the Dickinson. (*He shuts his eyes, reciting from memory, holding the book against his chest.*)

"There came a Wind like a Bugle—
It quivered through the Grass
And a Green Chill upon the Heat
So ominous did pass
We barred the Windows and the Doors
As from an Emerald Ghost—"

(*opens the book and starts riffling through it*) Let's see now, where's the rest . . . ? (*He finally finds it.*) Ahhh, here we go . . . !

FANNY. (*re-enters, drink in hand*) I'm back! (*takes one look at GARDNER and bursts out laughing again*)

MAGS. I don't believe you! How you can laugh at him . . . ?!

FANNY. I'm sorry, I wish I could stop, but there's really nothing else to do. Look at him . . . just . . . look at him . . . !

(*This is all simultaneous as MAGS gets angrier and angrier.*)

MAGS. It's so cruel . . . you're so . . . incredibly cruel to him . . . I mean, YOUR DISDAIN REALLY TAKES MY BREATH AWAY! YOU'RE IN A CLASS BY YOURSELF WHEN IT COMES TO HUMILIA-TION . . . !

GARDNER. (*reading*)
"The Doom's electric Moccasin
That very instant passed—
On a strange Mob of panting Trees
And Fences fled away
And Rivers where the Houses ran

Those looked that lived — that Day —
The Bell within the steeple wild
The flying tidings told —
How much can come
And much can go,
And yet abide the World!"
(*He shuts the book with a bang, pauses and looks around the room, confused.*) Now, where was I . . . ?

FANNY. Safe and sound in the middle of the living room with Mags and me.

GARDNER. But I was looking for something, wasn't I . . . ?

FANNY. Your manuscript.

GARDNER. THAT'S RIGHT! MY MANUSCRIPT! My manuscript!

FANNY. And here it is all over the floor. See, you're standing on it.

GARDNER. (*picks up a few pages and looks at them*) Why, so I am . . .

FANNY. Now all we have to do is get it up off the floor and packed neatly into these cartons!

GARDNER. Yes, yes, that's right. Into the cartons.

FANNY. (*kicks a carton over to him*) Here, you use this one and I'll start over here . . . (*She starts dropping papers into a carton nearby.*) . . . BOMBS AWAY . . . ! Hey . . . this is fun . . . !

GARDNER. (*picks up his own pile, lifts it high over his head and flings it down into the carton*) BOMBS AWAY . . . This *is* fun . . . !

FANNY. I told you! The whole thing is to figure out a system!

GARDNER. I don't know what I'd do without you, Fan. I thought I'd lost everything.

FANNY. (*makes dive bomber noises and machine gun*

explosions as she wheels more and more papers into the carton) TAKE THAT AND THAT AND THAT . . . !

GARDNER. (*joins in the fun, outdoing her with dips, dives and blastings of his own*) BLAM BLAM BLAM BLAM! . . . ZZZZZZZZRAAAAAA FOOM! . . . BLATTY DE BLATTY DE BLATTY DE KA-BOOOOOOOOM . . . ! WHAAAAAAA . . . DA DAT DAT DAT DAT . . . WHEEEEEEEE-AAAAAAAAAAAA . . . FOOOOOO . . . (*They get louder and louder as papers fly every which way.*)

FANNY. (*mimes getting hit with a bomb*) AEEEEEE-IIIIIIIIIIII! YOU GOT ME RIGHT IN THE GIZ-ZARD! (*She collapses on the floor and starts going through death throes, having an absolute ball.*)

GARDNER. TAKE THAT AND THAT AND THAT AND THAT . . . (*a series of explosions follow*)

MAGS. (*furious*) This is how you help him . . . ? THIS IS HOW YOU PACK HIS THINGS . . . ?

FANNY. I keep him company. I get involved . . . which is a hell of a lot more than you do!

MAGS. (*wild with rage*) BUT YOU'RE MAKING A MOCKERY OF HIM . . . YOU TREAT HIM LIKE A CHILD OR SOME DIM-WITTED SERVING BOY. HE'S JUST AN AMUSEMENT TO YOU . . . !

FANNY. (*Fatigue has finally overtaken her. She's calm to the point of serenity.*) . . . and to you who see him once a year, if that . . . What is he to *you?* . . . I mean, what do you give him from yourself that costs you something . . . ? Hmmmmmm . . . ? (*imitating her*) "Oh, hi Daddy, it's great to see you again. How have you been? . . . Gee, I love your hair. It's gotten so . . . *white!*" . . . What color do you expect it to get when he's this age . . . ? I mean, if you care so much how he looks, why don't you come and see him once in a while? . . . But oh no . . .

you have your paintings to do and your shows to put on.
You just come and see us when the whim strikes. (*imitating her*) "Hey, you know what would be really great?
. . . To do a portrait of you! I've always wanted to paint
you, you're such great subjects!" . . . *Paint* us . . . ?!
What about opening your eyes and really *seeing* us . . . ?
Noticing what's going on around here for a change! It's
all over Daddy and me. This is it! "Finita la commedia!"
. . . All I'm trying to do is exit with a little flourish,
have some fun . . . What's so terrible about that? . . .
It can get pretty grim around here, in case you haven't
noticed . . . Daddy, tap, tap tapping out his nonsense
all day; me traipsing around to the thrift shops trying to
amuse myself . . . He never keeps me company anymore, never takes me out anywhere . . . I'd put a bullet
through my head in a minute, but then who'd look after
him? . . . What do you think we're moving to the cottage for . . . ? So I can watch him like a hawk and make
sure he doesn't get lost. Do you think that's anything to
look forward to? . . . Being Daddy's nursemaid out in
the middle of nowhere? I'd much rather stay here in
Boston with the few friends I have left, but you can't
always do what you want in this world! "L'homme propose, Dieu dispose!" . . . If you want to paint us so
badly, you ought to paint us as we really are. There's
your picture . . . ! (*She points to GARDNER who's
quietly playing with a paper glider.*) . . . Daddy spread
out on the floor with all his toys and me hovering over
him to make sure he doesn't hurt himself! (*She
goes over to him.*) YOO HOO . . . GAR . . . ? . . .
HELLO? . . .

GARDNER. (*looks up at her*) Oh, hi there, Fan.
What's up?

FANNY. How's the packing coming . . . ?

GARDNER. Packing . . . ?

FANNY. Yes, you were packing your manuscript, remember? (*She lifts up a page and lets it fall into a carton.*)

GARDNER. Oh yes . . .

FANNY. Here's your picture, Mags. Face over this way . . . turn your easel over here . . . (*She lets a few more papers fall.*) Up, up . . . and away . . .

BLACKOUT

SCENE 2

The last day. All the books and boxes are gone. The room is completely empty except for MAGs' backdrop. Late afternoon light dapples the walls; it changes from pale peach to deeper violet. The finished portrait sits on the easel covered with a cloth. MAGS is taking down the backdrop.

FANNY. (*offstage to GARDNER*) DON'T FORGET TOOTS!

GARDNER. (*offstage from another part of the house*) WHAT'S THAT . . . ?

FANNY. (*offstage*) I SAID: DON'T FORGET TOOTS! HIS CAGE IS SITTING IN THE MIDDLE OF YOUR STUDY! (*silence*)

FANNY. (*offstage*)	GARDNER. (*offstage*)
HELLO . . . ? ARE	I'LL BE RIGHT WITH
ARE YOU THERE . . . ?	YOU, I'M JUST
	GETTING TOOTS!

GARDNER. (*offstage*) WHAT'S THAT? I CAN'T HEAR YOU?

FANNY. (*offstage*) I'M GOING THROUGH THE

ROOMS ONE MORE TIME TO MAKE SURE WE
DIDN'T FORGET ANYTHING . . . KITTY'S PICK-
ING US UP IN 15 MINUTES, SO PLEASE BE READY
. . . SHE'S DROPPING MAGS OFF AT THE STA-
TION AND THEN IT'S OUT TO ROUTE 3 AND THE
CAPE HIGHWAY . . .

GARDNER. (*enters, carrying Toots in his cage*) Well,
this is it. The big moment has finally come, eh what,
Toots? (*He sees MAGS.*) Oh hi there, Mags, I didn't see
you . . .

MAGS. Hi, daddy. I'm just taking this down . . . (*She
does and walks over to Toots.*) Oh Toots, I'll miss you.
(*She makes little chattering noises into his cage.*)

GARDNER. Come on, recite a little Grey's Elegy for
Mags before we go.

MAGS. Yes, Mum said he was really good at it now.

GARDNER. Well, the whole thing is to keep at it every
day. (*slowly to Toots*)
"The curfew tolls the knell of parting day,
The lowing herd wind slowly o'er the lea . . ."

Come on, show Mags your stuff!
(*slower*)
"The curfew tolls the knell of parting day,
The lowing herd wind slowly o'er the lea."
(*Silence; he makes little chattering sounds.*) Come on,
Toots, old boy . . .

MAGS. How does it go?

GARDNER. (*to MAGS*)
"The curfew tolls the knell of parting day,
The lowing herd wind slowly o'er the lea . . ."

MAGS. (*slowly to Toots*)
"The curfew tolls for you and me,
As quietly the herd winds down . . ."

GARDNER. No, no, it's: "The curfew tolls the knell of parting *day . . .* !

MAGS. (*repeating after him*) "The curfew tolls the knell of parting day . . ."

GARDNER. . . . "The lowing herd wind slowly o'er the lea . . ."

MAGS. (*with a deep breath*)
"The curfew tolls at parting day,
The herd low slowly down the lea . . . no, *knell!*
They come winding down the *knell* . . . !"

GARDNER. Listen, Mags . . . *listen!* (*a pause*)

TOOTS. (*loud and clear with GARDNER's inflection*)
"The curfew tolls the knell of parting day,
The lowing herd wind slowly o'er the lea,
The ploughman homeward plods his weary way,
And leaves the world to darkness and to me."

MAGS. HE SAID IT . . . HE SAID IT! . . . AND IN YOUR VOICE! . . . OH DADDY, THAT'S AMAZ-ING!

GARDNER. Well, Toots is very smart, which is more than I can say for alot of people I know . . .

MAGS. (*to Toots*) "Polly want a cracker? Polly want a cracker?"

GARDNER. You can teach a parakeet to say anything, all you need is patience . . .

MAGS. But *poetry* . . . that's so hard . . .

FANNY. (*Enters carrying a suitcase and GARDNER's typewriter in its case. She's dressed in her travelling suit wearing a hat to match.*) WELL, THERE YOU ARE! I THOUGHT YOU'D DIED!

MAGS. (*to FANNY*) He said it! I finally heard Toots recite Grey's Elegy. (*leaning close to the cage*) "Polly want a cracker? Polly want a cracker?"

FANNY. Isn't it uncanny how much he sounds like

Daddy? Sometimes when I'm alone here with him, I've actually thought he *was* Daddy and started talking to him. Oh yes, Toots and I have had quite a few meaty conversations together!

(*FANNY wolf whistles into the cage, then draws back. GARDNER covers the cage with a travelling cloth. Silence.*)

FANNY. (*looking around the room*) God, the place looks so bare.

MAGS. I still can't believe it . . . Cotuit, year round. I wonder if there'll be any phosphorous when you get there?

FANNY. What on earth are you talking about? (*spies the backdrop on the floor, carries it out to the hall*)

MAGS. Remember that summer when the ocean was full of phosphorus?

GARDNER. (*carrying Toots out into the hall*) Oh yes . . .

MAGS. It was a great mystery where it came from or why it settled in Cotuit. But one evening when Daddy and I were taking a swim, suddenly it was there!

GARDNER. (*returns*) I remember.

MAGS. I don't know where Mum was . . .

FANNY. (*re-enters*) Probably doing the dishes!

MAGS. (*to GARDNER*) As you dove into the water, this shower of silvery-green sparks erupted all around you. It was incredible! I thought you were turning into a saint or something, but then you told me to jump in too and the same thing happened to me . . .

GARDNER. Oh yes, I remember that . . . the water smelled all queer.

MAGS. What *is* phosphorus, anyway?

GARDNER. Chemicals, chemicals . . .

FANNY. No, it isn't. Phosphorus is a green liquid inside insects. Fireflies have it. When you see sparks in the water it means insects are swimming around . . .

GARDNER. Where on earth did you get that idea . . . ?

FANNY. If you're bitten by one of them, it's fatal!

MAGS. . . . and the next morning it was still there . . .

GARDNER. It was the damndest stuff to get off! We'd have to stay in the shower a good ten minutes. It comes from chemical waste, you see . . .

MAGS. Our bodies looked like mercury as we swam around . . .

GARDNER. It stained all the towels a strange yellow-green.

MAGS. I was in heaven, and so were you for that matter. You'd finished your day's poetry and would turn somersaults like some happy dolphin . . .

FANNY. Damned dishes . . . why didn't I see any of this . . . ?!

MAGS. I remember one night in particular . . . We sensed the phosphorus was about to desert us, blow off to another town. We were chasing each other under water. At one point I lost you the brilliance was so intense . . . but finally your foot appeared . . . then your leg. I grabbed it! . . . I remember wishing the moment would hold forever, that we could just be fixed there, laughing and irridescent . . . Then I began to get panicky because I knew it would pass, it was passing already. You were slipping from my grasp. The summer was almost over. I'd be going back to art school, you'd be going back to Boston . . . Even as I was reaching for you, you were gone. We'd never be like that again. (*silence*)

FANNY. (*spies MAGS' portrait covered on the easel*)

What's that over there? Don't tell me we forgot something!

MAGS. It's your portrait. I finished it.

FANNY. You finished it? How on earth did you manage that?

MAGS. I stayed up all night.

FANNY. You did? . . . *I* didn't hear you, did you hear her, Gar . . . ?

GARDNER. Not a peep, not a peep!

MAGS. Well, I wanted to get it done before you left. You know, see what you thought. It's not bad, considering . . . I mean, I did it almost completely from memory. The light was terrible and I was trying to be quiet so I wouldn't wake you. It was hardly an ideal situation . . . I mean, you weren't the most cooperative models . . . (*She suddenly panics and snatches the painting off the easel. She hugs it to her chest and starts dancing around the room with it.*) Oh God, you're going to hate it! You're going to hate it! How did I ever get into this? . . . Listen, you don't really want to see it . . . it's nothing . . . just a few dabs here and there . . . It was awfully late when I finished it. The light was really impossible and my eyes were hurting like crazy . . . Look, why don't we just go out to the sidewalk and wait for Kitty so she doesn't have to honk . . .

GARDNER. (*snatches the painting out from under her*) WOULD YOU JUST SHUT UP A MINUTE AND LET US SEE IT . . . ?

MAGS. (*laughing and crying*) But it's nothing, Daddy . . . *really!* . . . I've done better with my eyes closed! It was so late I could hardly see anything and then I spilled a whole bottle of thinner into my palette . . .

GARDNER. (*sets it down on the easel and stands back to look at it*) THERE!

MAGS. (*dancing around them in a panic*) Listen, it's just a quick sketch . . . It's still wet . . . I didn't have enough time . . . It takes at least 40 hours to do a decent portrait . . .

(*Suddenly it's very quiet as FANNY and GARDNER stand back to look at it.*)

MAGS. (*more and more beside herself, keeps leaping around the room wrapping her arms around herself, making little whimpering sounds*) Please don't . . . no . . . don't . . . oh please! . . . Come on, don't look . . . Oh God, don't . . . please . . . (*An eternity passes as FANNY and GARDNER gaze at it.*)

GARDNER. Well . . .

FANNY. Well . . . (*more silence*)

FANNY. I think it's   GARDNER. Awfully
perfectly dreadful!   clever, awfully clever!

FANNY. What on earth did you do to my face . . . ?

GARDNER. I particularly like Mum!

FANNY. Since when do I have purple skin . . . ?!

MAGS. I told you it was nothing, just a silly . . .

GARDNER. She looks like a million dollars!

FANNY. AND WILL YOU LOOK AT MY HAIR . . . IT'S BRIGHT ORANGE!

GARDNER. (*views it from another angle*) It's really very good!

FANNY. (*pointing*) That doesn't look anything like me!

GARDNER. . . . first rate!

FANNY. Since when do I have purple skin and bright orange hair . . . ?!

MAGS. (*trying to snatch it off the easel*) Listen, you don't have to worry about my feelings . . . really . . . I . . .

GARDNER. (*blocking her way*) NOT SO FAST . . .

FANNY. . . . and look at how I'm sitting! I've never sat like that in my life!

GARDNER. (*moving closer to it*) Yes, yes, it's awfully clever . . .

FANNY. I HAVE NO FEET!

GARDNER. The whole thing is quite remarkable!

FANNY. And what happened to my legs, pray tell? . . . They just vanish below the knees! . . . At least my dress is presentable. I've always loved that dress.

GARDNER. It sparkles somehow . . .

FANNY. (*to GARDNER*) Don't you think it's becoming?

GARDNER. Yes, very becoming, awfully becoming . . .

FANNY. (*examining it at closer range*) Yes, she got the dress very well, how it shows off what's left of my figure . . . My smile is nice too.

GARDNER. Good and wide . . .

FANNY. I love how the corners of my mouth turn up . . .

GARDNER. It's very clever . . .

FANNY. They're almost quivering . . .

GARDNER. Good lighting effects!

FANNY. Actually, I look quite . . . *young,* don't you think?

GARDNER. (*to MAGS*) You're awfully good with those highlights.

FANNY. (*looking at it from different angles*) And *you* look darling . . . !

GARDNER. Well, I don't know about that . . .

FANNY. No, you look absolutely darling. Good enough to eat!

MAGS. (*in a whisper*) They like it . . . They like it! (*A silence as FANNY and GARDNER keep gazing at it!*)

FANNY. You know what it is? The whispy brush

strokes make us look like a couple in a French Impressionist painting.

GARDNER. Yes, I see what you mean . . .

FANNY. . . . a Manet or Renoir . . .

GARDNER. It's very evocative.

FANNY. There's something about the light . . . (*They back up to survey it from a distance.*) You know those Renoir café scenes . . . ?

GARDNER. She doesn't lay on the paint with a trowel, it's just touches here and there . . .

MAGS. They *like* it . . . !

FANNY. You know the one with the couple dancing . . . ? Not that we're dancing. There's just something similar in the mood . . . a kind of gaity, almost . . . The man has his back to you and he's swinging the woman around . . . OH GAR, YOU'VE SEEN IT A MILLION TIMES! IT'S HANGING IN THE MUSEUM OF FINE ARTS! . . . They're dancing like this . . . (*She goes up to him and puts an arm on his shoulder.*)

MAGS. They like it . . . they like it!

FANNY. She's got on this wonderful flowered dress with ruffles at the neck and he's holding her like this . . . that's right . . . and she's got the most rhapsodic expression on her face . . .

GARDNER. (*getting into the spirit of it, takes FANNY in his arms and slowly begins to dance around the room*) Oh yes . . . I know the one you mean . . . They're in a sort of haze . . . and isn't there a little band playing off to one side . . . ?

FANNY. Yes, that's it!

(*Kitty's horn honks outside.*)

MAGS. (*is the only one who hears it*) There's Kitty! (*She's torn and keeps looking towards the door, but finally can't take her eyes off their stolen dance.*)

FANNY. . . . and there's a man in a dark suit playing the violin and someone's conducting, I think . . . And aren't Japanese lanterns strung up . . . ? (*They pick up speed, dipping and whirling around the room. Strains of a far-away Chopin waltz are heard.*)

GARDNER. Oh yes! There are all these little lights twinkling in the trees . . .

FANNY. . . . and doesn't the woman have a hat on . . . ? A big red hat . . . ?

GARDNER. . . . and lights all over the dancers too. Everything shimmers with this marvelous glow. Yes, yes . . . I can see it perfectly! The whole thing is absolutely extraordinary! (*The lights become dreamy and dappled as they dance around the room. MAGS watches them, moved to tears and . . .*)

THE CURTAIN FALLS

MUSIC IN THE PLAY

During the scene changes the opening measures of the following Chopin waltzes are played:

— As the house lights dim, the Waltz in A minor, opus posthumous.
— Setting up Act I, Scene 2, the Waltz in E minor, opus posthumous.
— Setting up Act I, Scene 3, the Waltz in E major, opus posthumous.
— To close Act I, the final notes of the Waltz in B minor, opus 69, #2.
— As the house lights dim for Act II, the Waltz in A flat major, opus 64, #3.
— Setting up Act II, Scene 2, repeat the Waltz in A minor, opus posthumous.
— To accompany the final moments of GARDNER's and FANNY's dance, the Waltz in D flat major, opus 70, #3.

WARDROBE PLOT

ACT ONE

Scene 1

FANNY
  White full slip
  Pink Bathrobe
  Blue Slippers
  Red Feathered Hat
  Aqua Dress w/red Brooch
  Taupe shoes
GARDNER
  Eyeglasses
  Watch
  Brown Wing tips
  Mauve Brown pants w/suspenders
  White shirt
  Bow tie
  Brown cardigan
  Plaid bathrobe
MAGS
  Dk. Grey pants
  Aqua shirt
  Blue Sweater shirt
  Lavender socks
  Black boots

Scene 2

FANNY
  Purple flowered dress w/fan Brooch
  Green hat
  Brown shoes

GARDNER
    Greenish brown tweed pants w/suspenders
    Brown sweater vest
    Checked wool jacket
    Striped tie
    Raincoat
MAGS
    Lt. Grey cord pants
    Blue Sweater shirt
    Beaded neck band

Scene 3

FANNY
    Navy & White dress
    Pink & Black hat
GARDNER
    Same pants & shirt as Sc. 2
    3 Ties
    Plaid Wool scarf
    Hawaiian shirt
    Purple College sweater
    Brown sweater vest
    Checked wool jacket
MAGS
    Lt. Grey cords
    Purple T-shirt
    Grey baseball shirt

ACT TWO

Scene 1

FANNY
    Black velvet dress
    Black pumps

Black hat
Black long gloves
Pearl earrings
Pearl necklace
GARDNER
Black Tuxedo
Black bow tie
Black cummerbund
White shirt w/snap on tux shirt front
Black patent shoes
MAGS
White painted T-shirt
Grey sweatpants-painted
Black chinese slippers

Scene 2

FANNY
Lavender suit
Floral scarf
Grey hat
Beige purse
White gloves — nylon
GARDNER
Brown suit
Corduroy vest
Bow tie
Brown Wing tips
MAGS
Dk. Grey pants
Aqua shirt
Black boots

PROP PLOT

FURNITURE
1 loveseat
1 armchair — castered
1 small end table
2 posing chairs
1 footstool
1 kitchen step ladder
1 standing lamp w/shade

PACKING BOXES
1 wardrobe
8 small boxes (13″ × 13″ × 18″)
6 med. boxes (18″ × 18″ × 20″) NOTE: 2 of these should
  be attached w/lid that covers both
All boxes should be marked with a Boston or World-
  wide moving company's name
6 furniture dollies — covered w/plywood and carpeting.
  Tops meas. 20″ × 40″

PROPS

ACT ONE

Scene 1

1 sheet — double bed size
2 packing blankets
5 lg. apothecary jars — hung from ceiling NOTE: 1 is
  a *magic* jar rigged for special effects.
3 shades for windows
1 table lamp
1 lamp shade — hand colored w/scene of Grand Canal

1 wood box—holds silver set
1 set of silver including:
  Tray
  Coffee urn
  Coffee pot
  Tea pot
Set of cloth covers—for silver
1 5x7 yellow tablet
1 pencil—attached to pad w/string
1 sm. box of antique teaspoons
Stack of papers—3″ of 8½ × 11″—4 to 6 lines of poems ea.
1 sm. leather suitcase—with Mags
1 duffle bag—lg. enough to hold easel & paint box
1 portable easel—easy to set up—wood
1 paint box—tackle box type—should hold brushes, etc.
Assorted brushes—in paint box
Assorted rags—in paint box
1 sm tube ea. of red, yellow, blue, green, and violet
  paint—all should be water-based Guasche or Grease-
  paint
1 lg. tube of white paint
1 lg. rag—lg. enough to cover footstool
Several sticks of sketching charcoal
Box of saltines—unsalted tops, several eaten
Crash box—noise from study, books not glass

Scene 2

Lg. wicker basket w/lid—old picnic type—holds pots &
  pans
Assorted kitchen pans—in wicker basket
1 old sm. trunk
Assorted tablecloths & linens—attached to trunk

1 lg. crimson tablecloth
1 pr. rubber galoshes
½ tin of Sara Lee Banana Cake
1 teaspoon — to eat cake
1 wooden handled hammer
1 box nails
2 wooden clothes hangers
8 7 oz. drink glasses
Bucket of ice & tongs — offstage — to make drinks
Bottle of water — offstage for actors to make drinks
Bottle of Cran-apple Juice — offstage for drinks
   (Dubonnet)
1 serving fork

Scene 3

Assorted old clothes — to be folded & packed in boxes
Assorted hat boxes
Assorted clothing storage boxes
1 shoe tree
Assorted mens & womens shoes — for shoe tree
Kodak or Polaroid camera & film — type that develops
   pics instantly, should always flash
1 opaque bowl — holds tapioca pudding
Tapioca pudding
1 teaspoon

ACT TWO

Scene 1

1 10′ × 20′ drop cloth — painted same as floor
1 blank canvas — 14″ × 24″, covered w/unprinted
   newsprint to be sketched on

Blank newsprint
1 chamois cloth
60 books—3 stacks green, 1 stack maroon, 3 stacks
   mixed
1 sm. striped book
1 sm. dusty black book
1 sm. book of collected poems
20″ of typing paper—bits of poems typed on ea. page.
   15 to 20 ruined ea.
Bowl w/warm water—offstage to wet actors pants
Sponge—offstage to wet actors pants

Scene 2

1 canvas w/finished portrait—11″x17″
1 white cloth cover for canvas
1 bird cage—rigged on bottom for casette recorder to
   be attached
1 blue parakeet
Cloth cover for bird cage
1 lg. suitcase
1 sm. black typewriter case—portable type

ADDITIONS & DRESSING

1 hall oriental rug
1 lg. mirror for mantle
Assorted packing labels & tags for boxes & furniture
Dressing to be decided upon w/designer
Manual typewriter
Pipe
Cloth for lamp shade

Other Publications for Your Interest

A WEEKEND NEAR MADISON

(LITTLE THEATRE—COMIC DRAMA)

By KATHLEEN TOLAN

2 men, 3 women—Interior

This recent hit from the famed Actors Theatre of Louisville, a terrific ensemble play about male-female relationships in the 80's, was praised by *Newsweek* as "warm, vital, glowing . . . full of wise ironies and unsentimental hopes". The story concerns a weekend reunion of old college friends now in their early thirties. The occasion is the visit of Vanessa, the queen bee of the group, who is now the leader of a lesbian/feminist rock band. Vanessa arrives at the home of an old friend who is now a psychiatrist hand in hand with her naif-like lover, who also plays in the band. Also on hand are the psychiatrist's wife, a novelist suffering from writer's block; and his brother, who was once Vanessa's lover and who still loves her. In the course of the weekend, Vanessa reveals that she and her lover desperately want to have a child—and she tries to persuade her former male lover to father it, not understanding that he might have some feelings about the whole thing. *Time Magazine* heard "the unmistakable cry of an infant hit . . . Playwright Tolan's work radiates promise and achievement." (#25051)

PASTORALE

(LITTLE THEATRE—COMEDY)

By DEBORAH EISENBERG

3 men, 4 women—Interior
(plus 1 or 2 bit parts and 3 optional extras)

"Deborah Eisenberg is one of the freshest and funniest voices in some seasons."—Newsweek. Somewhere out in the country Melanie has rented a house and in the living room she, her friend Rachel who came for a weekend but forgets to leave, and their school friend Steve (all in their mid-20s) spend nearly a year meandering through a mental landscape including such concerns as phobias, friendship, work, sex, slovenliness and epistemology. Other people happen by: Steve's young girlfriend Celia, the virtuous and annoying Edie, a man who Melanie has picked up in a bar, and a couple who appear during an intense conversation and observe the sofa is on fire. The lives of the three friends inevitably proceed and eventually draw them, the better prepared perhaps by their months on the sofa, in separate directions. "The most original, funniest new comic voice to be heard in New York theater since Beth Henley's 'Crimes of the Heart.'"—N.Y. Times. "A very funny, stylish comedy."—The New Yorker. "Wacky charm and wayward wit."—New York Magazine. "Delightful."—N.Y. Post. "Uproarious . . . the play is a world unto itself, and it spins."—N.Y. Sunday Times. (#18016)

Other Publications for Your Interest

TALKING WITH . . .
(LITTLE THEATRE)
By JANE MARTIN

11 women—Bare stage

Here, at last, is the collection of eleven extraordinary monologues for eleven actresses which had them on their feet cheering at the famed Actors Theatre of Louisville—audiences, critics and, yes, even jaded theatre professionals. The mysteriously pseudonymous Jane Martin is truly a "find", a new writer with a wonderfully idiosyncratic style, whose characters alternately amuse, move and frighten us always, however, speaking to us from the depths of their souls. The characters include a baton twirler who has found God through twirling; a fundamentalist snake handler, an ex-rodeo rider crowded out of the life she has cherished by men in 3-piece suits who want her to dress up "like Minnie damn Mouse in a tutu"; an actress willing to go to any length to get a job; and an old woman who claims she once saw a man with "cerebral walrus" walk into a McDonald's and be healed by a Big Mac. "Eleven female monologues, of which half a dozen verge on brilliance."—London Guardian. "Whoever (Jane Martin) is, she's a writer with an original imagination."—Village Voice. "With Jane Martin, the monologue has taken on a new poetic form, intensive in its method and revelatory in its impact."—Philadelphia Inquirer. "A dramatist with an original voice . . . (these are) tales about enthusiasms that become obsessions, eccentric confessionals that levitate with religious symbolism and gladsome humor."—N.Y. Times. *Talking With* . . . is the 1982 winner of the American Theatre Critics Association Award for Best Regional Play. (#22009)

HAROLD AND MAUDE
(ADVANCED GROUPS—COMEDY)
By COLIN HIGGINS

9 men, 8 women—Various settings

Yes: *the Harold and Maude!* This is a stage adaptation of the wonderful movie about the suicidal 19 year-old boy who finally learns how to truly *live* when he meets up with that delightfully whacky octogenarian, Maude. Harold is the proverbial Poor Little Rich Kid. His alienation has caused him to attempt suicide several times, though these attempts are more cries for attention than actual attempts. His peculiar attachment to Maude, whom he meets at a funeral (a mutual passion), is what saves him—and what captivates us. This new stage version, a hit in France directed by the internationally-renowned Jean-Louis Barrault, will certainly delight both afficionados of the film and new-comers to the story. "Offbeat upbeat comedy."—Christian Science Monitor. (#10032)

Other Publications for Your Interest

AGNES OF GOD
(LITTLE THEATRE—DRAMA)

By JOHN PIELMEIER

3 women—1 set (bare stage)

Doctor Martha Livingstone, a court-appointed psychiatrist, is asked to determine the sanity of a young nun accused of murdering her own baby. Mother Miriam Ruth, the nun's superior, seems bent on protecting Sister Agnes from the doctor, and Livingstone's suspicions are immediately aroused. In searching for solutions to various mysteries (who killed the baby? Who fathered the child?) Livingstone forces all three women, herself included, to face some harsh realities in their own lives, and to re-examine the meaning of faith and the commitment of love. "Riveting, powerful, electrifying new drama . . . three of the most magnificent performances you will see this year on any stage anywhere . . . the dialogue crackles."—Rex Reed, N.Y. Daily News. ". . . outstanding play . . . deals intelligently with questions of religion and psychology."—Mel Gussow, N.Y. Times. ". . . unquestionably blindingly theatrical . . . cleverly executed blood and guts evening in the theatre . . . three sensationally powered performances calculated to wring your withers."—Clive Barnes, N.Y. Post.   (#236)

(Posters available)

COME BACK TO THE 5 & DIME, JIMMY DEAN, JIMMY DEAN
(ADVANCED GROUPS—DRAMA)

By ED GRACZYK

1 man, 8 women—Interior

In a small-town dime store in West Texas, the Disciples of James Dean gather for their twentieth reunion. Now a gaggle of middle-aged women, the Disciples were teenagers when Dean filmed "Giant" two decades ago in nearby Marfa. One of them, an extra in the film, has a child whom she says was conceived by Dean on the "Giant" set; the child is the Jimmy Dean of the title. The ladies' reminiscences mingle with flash-backs to their youth; then the arrival of a stunning and momentarily unrecognized woman sets off a series of confrontations that upset their self-deceptions and expose their well-hidden disappointments. "Full of homespun humor . . . surefire comic gems."—N.Y. Post. "Captures convincingly the atmosphere of the 1950s."—Women's Wear Daily.   (#5147)

Other Publications for Your Interest

SEA MARKS

(LITTLE THEATRE—DRAMA)

By GARDNER McKAY

1 woman, 1 man—Unit set

Winner of L.A. Drama Critics Circle Award "Best Play." This is the "funny, touching, bittersweet tale" (Sharbutt, A.P.) of a fisherman living on a remote island to the west of Ireland who has fallen in love with, in retrospect, a woman he's glimpsed only once. Unschooled in letter-writing, he tries his utmost to court by mail and, after a year-and-a-half, succeeds in arranging a rendezvous at which, to his surprise, she persuades him to live with her in Liverpool. Their love affair ends only when he is forced to return to the life he better understands. "A masterpiece." (The Tribune, Worcester, Mass.) "Utterly winning," (John Simon, New York Magazine.) "There's abundant humor, surprisingly honest humor, that grows between two impossible partners. The reaching out and the fearful withdrawal of two people who love each other but whose lives simply cannot be fused: a stubborn, decent, attractive and touching collision of temperments, honest in portraiture and direct in speech. High marks for SEA MARKS!" (Walter Kerr, New York Times.) "Fresh as a May morning. A lovely, tender and happily humorous love story." (Elliot Norton, Boston Herald American.) "It could easily last forever in actors' classrooms and audition studios." (Oliver, The New Yorker)

THE WOOLGATHERER

(LITTLE THEATRE—DRAMA)

By WILLIAM MASTROSIMONE

1 man, 1 woman—Interior

In a dreary Philadelphia apartment lives Rose, a shy and slightly creepy five-and-dime salesgirl. Into her life saunters Cliff, a hard-working, hard-drinking truck driver—who has picked up Rose and been invited back to her room. Rose is an innocent whose whole life centers around reveries and daydreams. He is rough and witty—but it's soon apparent—just as starved for love as she is. This little gem of a play was a recent success at New York's famed Circle Repertory starring Peter Weller and Patricia Wettig. Actors take note: *The Woolgatherer* has several excellent monologues. ". . . energy, compassion and theatrical sense are there."—N.Y. Times. ". . . another emotionally wrenching experience no theatre enthusiast should miss."—Rex Reed. "Mastrosimone writes consistently witty and sometimes lyrical dialogue."—New York Magazine. "(Mastrosimone) has a knack for composing wildly humorous lines at the same time that he is able to penetrate people's hearts and dreams."—Hollywood Reporter.

NEW
OFF-BROADWAY HITS

from
SAMUEL FRENCH, INC.

AFTER CRYSTAL NIGHT — ALTERATIONS —
THE ARTIFICIAL JUNGLE — BE HAPPY
FOR ME — THE BEACH HOUSE — BLUEBEARD —
CINDERELLA WALTZ — CROSSING
DELANCEY — DENNIS — THE EARLY GIRL —
EL SALVADOR — EPISODE 26 — EYES
OF THE AMERICAN — HOUSE ARREST —
HUNTING COCKROACHES — I LOVE YOU,
I LOVE YOU NOT — MAGGIE MAGALITA —
MAN ENOUGH — A MAP OF THE WORLD —
THE MYSTERY OF IRMA VEP — NEON
PSALMS — THE NORMAL HEART — NOT
SHOWING — PSYCHO BEACH PARTY —
ROSE COTTAGES — SEASCAPE WITH
SHARKS AND DANCER — STAGE BLOOD —
STOPPING THE DESERT — TALK RADIO —
TIMES SQUARE ANGEL — TOMORROW'S
MONDAY — VAMPIRE LESBIANS OF SODOM

Consult our most recent Catalogue for details.